Rochester
MEMORIES
VOLUME II ~ The 1940s, '50s & '60s

Acknowledgments

The *Democrat and Chronicle* is pleased to present *Rochester Memories, Volume II.*

This unique book is the result of contributions made by many people and organizations from throughout our readership area.

We are indebted to the many individuals who are committed to preserving our history in various libraries, archives and personal collections all around this area we call home.

In addition to the precious selections from family albums of many of our readers, we also received the generous contributions of time and access to photo archives from the Local History Division of the Central Library of Rochester and Monroe County, and the Rochester Historical Society.

This project also relied heavily on the archives of the *Democrat and Chronicle*. Our thanks go to the *Democrat and Chronicle* staff involved in this project including Jim Fogler, vice president/market development; Dennis Floss, director/marketing communications; project copy editor, Laura Nichols, assistant multimedia editor/production; Gini Wheeler, assistant data desk manager; and members of the Rochester Information Center's Diversity Committee, Diana Louise Carter and Mary Chao.

Published by Pediment Publishing, a division of The Pediment Group, Inc. www.pediment.com Printed in Canada

Foreword

The era from 1940 to 1969 brought, arguably, more change to the world than any other modern era. On the world stage and back at home, Rochesterians had a role to play in shaping that change.

Human conflict marked the three decades. The 1940s saw Americans unified in our fight against a common enemy, sending our sons and daughters off to the biggest war the world had ever known. Just 30 years later, the 1960s closed with Americans divided over the war in Southeast Asia, in addition to cultural and racial disagreements on the streets of American cities.

These 30 years were also marked by human innovation that on one end gave us the technology to obliterate our entire planet, and on the other end saw human beings set foot on another celestial body.

For 176 years, the *Democrat and Chronicle* has been telling the story of Rochester and its citizens, day in and day out. Yet, *Rochester Memories, Volume II* is a pictorial retrospective that is more than the newspaper's first rough draft of history. What makes this book unique is that many of its photos have been contributed by Rochesterians who opened up albums (and shoeboxes) to share their precious memories.

Come with us as we venture back to our not-so-distant past. Along the way, I trust you'll see some familiar faces and become acquainted with others who helped make Rochester into the community it is today. Enjoy!

Ali M. Zoibi
President & Publisher, *Democrat and Chronicle*

Table of Contents

Early History

Rochester, known in the early 19th century as the "Young Lion of the West," was America's first boomtown. With the Genesee River providing power and the Erie Canal access, by 1840 Rochester was known as "The Flour City," the largest flour-producing city in the United States. Ever adapting, Rochester became "The Flower City" and home to a flourishing nursery business as flour milling moved west.

In the mid-19th century, Rochester was an epicenter for social reform. Frederick Douglass founded the abolitionist newspaper *The North Star* here in 1847. A contemporary of Douglass, Susan B. Anthony, began fighting for civil rights as an abolitionist, and later her home in Rochester became a cradle of the women's rights movement.

Rochester saw another boom in the years after the Civil War. Eastman Kodak Co. and Bausch & Lomb were founded and put Rochester on the map as the world capital of expanding photographic and imaging industry.

George Eastman's legacy extended far beyond photography. The "Flower City" had weathered the Great Depression due to a strong economic base and Eastman's philanthropic and civic vision. By 1940, Rochester was the 23rd largest city in the United States, and one of the most livable in the nation. Those characteristics set the stage for another post-war boom.

LEFT: Box manufacturing department at Eastman Kodak Co. in Rochester, 1906. *Courtesy Democrat and Chronicle archives*

ABOVE: Court Street Bridge looking west, Rochester, late 1800s. *Courtesy Rochester Historical Society*

RIGHT: Stutson House on Stutson Street, Charlotte, circa 1876. *Courtesy Rochester Historical Society*

OPPOSITE TOP LEFT: A portrait of Susan B. Anthony, suffragist, 1820-1906. She was an American reformer and advocate of women's rights. She crusaded for temperance and the abolition of slavery, but is best known for her work in the national woman's suffrage movement, which culminated in the passage of the 19th Amendment to the Constitution in 1920. She lived in Rochester for many years, and her home at 17 Madison St. was a headquarters for the work of woman suffrage. This portrait was made by John H. Kent between 1870 and 1879. *Courtesy Local History Division, Central Library of Rochester and Monroe County*

OPPOSITE BOTTOM LEFT: Brininstool (known then as Briminstool) farms on River Road in Henrietta. *Courtesy Democrat and Chronicle archives*

OPPOSITE RIGHT: A portrait of Frederick Douglass, one of the 19th century's most famous African Americans. He was born into slavery in Maryland as Frederick Augustus Washington Bailey. His mother was a slave and it was suspected his father was his master. The master's wife taught Frederick how to read and write, an uncommon practice for slaves. Frederick escaped and changed his name to Frederick Douglass. He became an ardent abolitionist and was a highly sought-after lecturer. He moved to Rochester in 1847 and published The North Star, an African-American anti-slavery newspaper. In addition to his paper he was involved in the Underground Railroad, was a political adviser, diplomat, and a U.S. Marshall. Although he moved to Washington, D.C., in 1872, he was buried in Rochester after his death in 1895. This portrait is by John H. Kent, whose studio was at 20 State St. in Rochester The photograph was made between 1879 and 1883. *Courtesy Local History Division, Central Library of Rochester and Monroe County*

ABOVE: Osburn House, South St. Paul Street (South Avenue), Rochester, late 1800s.
Courtesy Rochester Historical Society

RIGHT: Plymouth Congretational Church, at the northeast corner of Troup Sreet and South Plymouth Avenue.
Courtesy Local History Division, Central Library of Rochester and Monroe County

BELOW: Innovative Ithaca architect William Miller designed this eclectic residence at 963 East Ave. for Judge Francis Macomber in 1888. It is one of three distinctive houses that Miller created for prominent families on East Avenue, the city's most prestigious residential area for more than 100 years. *Courtesy Landmark Society*

ABOVE: Electricity vs steam. The Rochester and Eastern Rapid Railway and the Auburn branch of the New York Central and Hudson River Railroad parallel each other between Rochester and Canandaigua, with the trains of each road running at full speed in the same direction. The electric car here is capable of making a speed of 60 miles per hour. This photo was taken during the race between the two in 1904.
Courtesy Democrat and Chronicle archives

TOP LEFT: The third Monroe County Courthouse, located on the southeast corner of Main and Fitzhugh streets, was designed by Rochester architect J. Foster Warner. Today, it is known as the Monroe County Office Building. *Courtesy Local History Division, Central Library of Rochester and Monroe County*

BOTTOM LEFT: Fire department pumper, Rochester, late 1800s.
Courtesy Local History Division, Central Library of Rochester and Monroe County

BELOW: Students from Ellwanger and Barry School No. 24 on Meigs Street in Rochester. It was named after George Ellwanger and Patrick Barry, the founders of Mount Hope Nurseries, which at one time was the largest in the world. They are responsible in part for Rochester earning the name "The Flower City." *Courtesy Rochester Historical Society*

LEFT: Eastside Savings Bank on Clinton Avenue and East Main Street, Rochester, early 1900s. *Courtesy Democrat and Chronicle archives*

OPPOSITE: View of State Street from Main Street, Rochester, circa 1910. *Courtesy Local History Division, Central Library of Rochester and Monroe County*

Views & Street Scenes

The temptation to compare the views in these photos with those same sites today is unavoidable. Even without cars in the photos, the automobile dominates the street scenes of Rochester during the 1940s, '50s and '60s.

The pedestrian traffic of previous decades – while bustling by today's standards – is noticeably absent. In views of downtown, the buildings are familiar, especially in the views before the urban renewal of the 1960s. But the streets, seen without trolleys, show cars and people in a standoff, each seemingly waiting for the other to move. Each of the street views on pages 20 and 21 show variations on this pas de deux.

Aerial views of Rochester drive the point home.

Roadways, freshly poured or paved, follow the paths laid by previous modes of transportation and reflect light in such a way that they look like slightly tamed versions of the Genesee River.

Seen from the air, the urban renewal is easier to spot. Clusters of dense rectangles – buildings and homes – have been cleared for roads or redevelopment projects, a little like shaved patches of skin, waiting for something to grow back.

LEFT: Aerial view of Rochester on April 25, 1963. Rochester's three major construction projects in 1963: Baden-Ormond redevelopment (just above right of center); cleared right-of-way for the final segment of the Inner Loop (lower right); and the Civic Center (lower left). Clinton Avenue is the most prominent vertically running street at center, with Midtown rising just to the right of it in the photo's lower half. Eastman Kodak Co. office tower is at far left center. Eleven bridges, or crossings, including Main Street, over the Genesee River can be seen. *Courtesy Local History Division, Central Library of Rochester and Monroe County*

ABOVE: The Stutson Street Bridge shows through the mist in Charlotte in 1940. *Courtesy Reyton Wojnowski*

TOP RIGHT: A mandatory fuel saving holiday occurred on Feb. 4, 1945. This is Main Street looking west. *Courtesy Eric Iversen*

BOTTOM RIGHT: A packet boat is drawn on the river around King's Bend, west of Pittsford, near the Sutherland Woods, circa 1945. *Courtesy Democrat and Chronicle archives*

BELOW: View of the Liberty Bridge, erected over Main Street in support of the troops and to collect war bond money, circa 1943. *Courtesy Local History Division, Central Library of Rochester and Monroe County*

ABOVE: View of the University of Rochester, circa 1945. *Courtesy Rochester Historical Society*

TOP: Bird's-eye view of the Genesee River and Upper Falls, circa 1940. *Courtesy Rochester Historical Society*

LEFT: The Taylor Building on the corner of Main and Stillson streets, circa 1940. *Courtesy Democrat and Chronicle archives*

ABOVE: The pavement of Main Street, paled by salt heaped on by municipal employees in the snowfall in December 1947. Apparently, the city was rather eager to avert traffic tie-ups such as the snow had caused in 1944 and 1945.
Courtesy Democrat and Chronicle archives

RIGHT: Aerial view of downtown Rochester in November 1951.
Courtesy Local History Division, Central Library of Rochester and Monroe County

BELOW: An aerial view of Rochester in September 1949.
Courtesy Local History Division, Central Library of Rochester and Monroe County

ABOVE: At Ides Cove on the west shore of Irondequoit Bay, where most of the buildings were year-round homes. The cove had deep, well-protected water. On the right, not shown, is Point Pleasant and its well-known old hotel. The spot is about a fourth of the bay length from Sea Breeze.
Courtesy Democrat and Chronicle archives

LEFT: This building on E Main and Swan streets was scheduled to be razed by the University of Rochester, its new owner, in July 1961. *Courtesy Democrat and Chronicle archives*

ABOVE: On this block, within a few weeks from when this photo was taken on March 23, 1962, 16 acres of land would be cleared in the Baden-Ormond area. The city would retain the strip across the center, on the south side of Kelly Street. The parcel above it, at right, was a proposed shopping center site. The industrial zone below the strip is divided into four parcels. The flat building in the center is the Sibley garage. Chatham Gardens apartments were scheduled to go up in left. *Courtesy Democrat and Chronicle archives*

TOP LEFT: View down Main Street and the W.T. Grant Co. building, circa 1959. *Courtesy Democrat and Chronicle Aachives*

LEFT: View of Joseph Avenue, 1964. Cohen's Restaurant, a pillar of the business area, is at left. *Courtesy Democrat and Chronicle archives*

FAR LEFT: View down Main Street in Fairport, 1967. *Courtesy Democrat and Chronicle archives*

ABOVE: The New York State Legislature authorized construction of a bridge over Irondequoit Bay in 1942, but the bridge would finally reach completion a year after this photo was taken in 1968. The bridge, a 2,317-foot structure, would span the bay. At this point two-thirds of the concrete roadway had been poured on a galvanized steel base, which rested on 20 concrete piles. *Courtesy Democrat and Chronicle archives*

LEFT: Facing easterly, this photo shows progress on the Irondequoit Bay bridge in November 1966. *Courtesy Democrat and Chronicle archives*

BELOW: View of the Inner Loop in Rochester, 1967. *Courtesy Local History Division, Central Library of Rochester and Monroe County*

ABOVE: View of the Western Expressway, looking east, Sept. 22, 1966. ABC Demolition Corp. of Arlington, N.Y, was the lowest of five bidders at $251,610 for razing 260 buildings along the Western Expressway between Mount Read Boulevard and Broad Street. The cost of the work had been estimated at $311,000. Rochester Atlas Wrecking Co Inc. submitted the lowest of six bids to demolish 150 buildings along the route of the Keeler Street Expressway. The Atlas bid was $203,495, compared with an estimate of $261,000. *Courtesy Local History Division, Central Library of Rochester and Monroe County*

LEFT: Keeler Street Expressway, 1969, just prior to its opening, which was scheduled for mid-October. This allowed motorists to travel from the Veterans Memorial Bridge to the Irondequoit Bay Bridge and the Sea Breeze neighborhood. *Courtesy Local History Division, Central Library of Rochester and Monroe County*

BELOW: View of downtown Rochester in June of 1964. *Courtesy Local History Division, Central Library of Rochester and Monroe County*

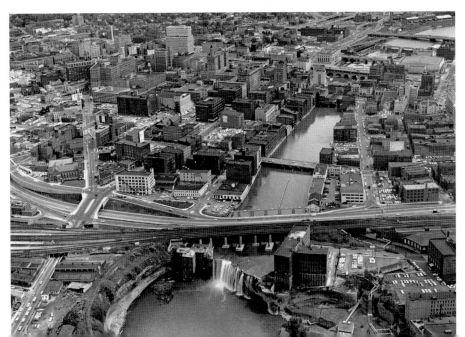

Transportation

The streets of Rochester in the 1940s held quite an array of conveyances. Buses, trains, bicycles and automobiles all shared the road with streetcars – at least until 1941, when the trolleys stopped rolling.

In the 1940s, the city had the distinction of being the smallest city in the world to have a subway system. Built in 1927 as a new "instrument for transportation and commerce" it ran for 8.25 miles following the route of the original Erie Canal. The subway never lived up to its potential and was discontinued in 1956, a victim of the rise of the automobile. Just a year later, construction of the Eastern Expressway (now known as Interstate 490) began in its place.

In 1940, the average cost of a new car was $850 – just about half the average annual income of $1,725. Gas cost 11 cents a gallon. In 1969, the average cost of a new car was $3,270, annual income was $8,540, and a gallon of gas was 35 cents.

By 1969, the car was clearly king of the road. Rochester was crisscrossed with ribbons of concrete and asphalt, none more complex than the "Can of Worms," which challenged generations of Rochester's drivers with its twisted merger of four major highways.

LEFT: Vida Gartland leading a tour around town on a Rochester Transit Corp. bus in 1951. *Courtesy Edward Gartland*

ABOVE: Intended to promote enlistments in naval aviation in Rochester, this Transit Corp. bus, decorated in red, white and blue at the company's own expense, went into regular passenger service on the Main Street line on Dec. 18, 1942. Herbert W. Cruickshank, right, associated member of the Naval Aviation Cadet Selection Board, Third Naval District, and John F. Uffert, vice president and general manager of the Rochester Transit Corp., are inspecting the vehicle. *Courtesy Democrat and Chronicle archives*

TOP: A steam engine train passes the Stutson Street Bridge, Charlotte in 1940. *Courtesy Reyton Wojnowski*

RIGHT: Don and Bob Feicht with their bicycles on Caroline Street in 1940. *Courtesy Ken and Mary Feicht*

ABOVE: Dewey Flowerday, home on leave from World War II, proudly stands by his Chevy with the torpedo back, Rochester, 1944.
Courtesy Diane Drysdale

TOP: Late in the evening of March 31, 1941, a crowd of 6,000 Rochesterians witnesses the end of streetcar service. The scene was near the corner of State and Main streets, looking north on State. The transit system "line car" is visible behind the street car, with workers ready to cut wires and begin dismantling the trolley service.
Courtesy Democrat and Chronicle archives

LEFT: Street car conductors in downtown Rochester, 1940.
Courtesy Ken and Mary Feicht

ABOVE: The Works Project Administration (WPA) was the largest New Deal agency, created by President Franklin D. Roosevelt, employing millions of people and affecting nearly every locality in the United States. These workers are at the Maple-Child tunnel in January 1941. *Courtesy Local History Division, Central Library of Rochester and Monroe County*

TOP: The Works Project Administration employing workers at St. Paul Street railway, circa 1945. *Courtesy Local History Division, Central Library of Rochester and Monroe County*

RIGHT: Rochester Transit Corp. trolley wire poles around town are salvaged, Sept. 28, 1942. There was only one machine capable of doing the job and it is shown here, with foreman Dan Olcott swinging off a cable attached to a pole just severed at its base. This photo was taken in front of the Times-Union Building as the crew moved south on Exchange Street. *Courtesy Local History Division, Central Library of Rochester and Monroe County*

ABOVE: Back view of the south side of the Main Street Bridge, one of the most famous and picturesque features of Rochester. The bridge, covered with buildings, is one of a few of its kind in the world. It has been compared by artists to the Ponte Vecchio in Florence, Italy. Colin Campbell Cooper and the late George Herdle, first director of the Memorial Art Gallery, painted pictures of it. The bridge was built in 1857. Buildings, some of them still standing, were erected on the north side of Main Street. The Ocumpaugh group, center of the south side, was presumed to have been erected in 1876. Picturesque or not, city planners and other citizens interested in the improvement of the downtown section did not like the old buildings in 1947. *Courtesy Local History Division, Central Library of Rochester and Monroe County*

BELOW: Ontario Car Ferry Co. reunion, held on April 20, 1950. From left, Percy H. Scott, manager, Ontario Car Ferry Co.; Samuel H. McCaig, Ontario II captain from 1907 to 1947; Charles Morrison, chief engineer for 23 years; and William Bryson, last captain of the vessel. *Courtesy Local History Division, Central Library of Rochester and Monroe County*

ABOVE: Ready to greet arriving passengers on the Capital Airways airliner *Rochester*, the largest plane ever to land at the county's airport, is Mayor Samuel B. Dicker, left, as hostess Dodie Beale cuts the ribbon across the door. The ceremony marked the opening of regular nonstop service between Rochester and Washington by 31-ton, 50-passenger Douglas C-4s. *Courtesy Local History Division, Central Library of Rochester and Monroe County*

BELOW: Paul Spindler, left, 9, and Raymond Spindler, 12, with their bicycles at 202 Thorncliffe Drive in west Irondequoit, 1946. *Courtesy Paul B. Spindler*

ABOVE: Workers haul out a huge piece of locomotive using heavy-duty cables and a large crane, following an accident that derailed the train, plunging it into the Genesee River, in 1947.
Courtesy Democrat and Chronicle archives

BELOW: Commerce Department officials predicted a step up in service in 1948 and work crews sped up the replacement of track on Rochester's subway. Here, at work underground near the Times Square station, are foreman Dominick Bovenzi (front left) and head foreman Joseph Gatto (right), aiding a crew in jacking up a section of rail. They are working by the portable gas light shown in the foreground in December 1947.
Courtesy Local History Division, Central Library of Rochester and Monroe County

ABOVE: Passengers on board a bus in downtown Rochester, circa 1945. *Courtesy Democrat and Chronicle archives*

BELOW: A mother and child wait for the ferry to arrive, circa 1950.
Courtesy Local History Division, Central Library of Rochester and Monroe County

ABOVE: Closed more than a year for repairs, the Driving Park Avenue Bridge reopened in December 1952. Completion of the bridge was held up by a delay in the arrival of steel railings. Parked cars shown on the bridge belonged to workers on the construction job in September 1952. *Courtesy Local History Division, Central Library of Rochester and Monroe County*

TOP LEFT: Starting on May 24, 1952, buses were absent from curb-side steps during a 23-day strike. Scenes like this were common during this period, which caused headaches for motorists throughout the city. *Courtesy Democrat and Chronicle archives*

LEFT: As a strike by the Rochester Transit Corp. drivers and mechanics loomed, city officials and union men meet in hopes of coming to a resolution. From left are Councilman Lawrence G. Edenhofer, Vice Mayor Norman A. Kreckman and Councilman William A. Legg flanking City Manager Louis B. Cartwright. On the other side of the table are, from left, Ogden U. Pixley, James J. Gormley, Horace Pratt, Hyman Gould, Russell A. Gerling and James B. Deane, representatives of the union on May 1, 1952. *Courtesy Democrat and Chronicle archives*

ABOVE: Loaded with yard crewmen, one of New York Central's smoke-less diesels slides into a clean new diesel inspection house, which replaced the sooty roundhouse at the Atlantic-Culver yards. The ceremony on April 25, 1952, marked the complete dieselization of the Rochester yard and the end of the soot plague. *Courtesy Local History Division, Central Library of Rochester and Monroe County*

RIGHT: The State Street barn of the Rochester Transit Corp. in March 1954, would be abandoned by buses in June 1956. The barn was built in the 1800s as a home for trolleys. *Courtesy Democrat and Chronicle archives*

FAR RIGHT: This C-124 Globemaster drops in at The Rochester Monroe Airport on June 19, 1953, on Air Force business, and officials open it to public inspection. The huge plane, one of the world's largest, was the same type as the one that crashed in Japan the previous day, killing 129 people. The nature of the business that brought the plane to Rochester was unknown. *Courtesy Local History Division, Central Library of Rochester and Monroe County*

ABOVE: Rush-hour jam late Sept. 10, 1954, in the City Hall-Times Square station, a year or so before the subway channel would be eliminated. *Courtesy Democrat and Chronicle archives*

TOP RIGHT: At the wheel of the first bus to leave the barn at 3:59 a.m. May 24, 1952, was Lewis LeWright, on the regular Park-Lake run. He had been with Rochester Transit Corp., since 1911. *Courtesy Democrat and Chronicle archives*

BOTTOM RIGHT: Driver Morris Cohen gets an explanation from patrolman Robert Wolff as patrolman Carl Kannenberg and Jaycees' William Leet check tail lights at Broad Street and Lyell Avenue, one of four car inspection stations set up on April 6, 1953. *Courtesy Local History Division, Central Library of Rochester and Monroe County*

ABOVE: Airport visitors get a first look at one of the helicopters that would carry Mohawk Airlines passengers on short-haul schedules in May 1954. *Courtesy Democrat and Chronicle archives*

TOP LEFT: Mohawk First Officer Howard Landsman, right, gets set in a Link trainer for a monthly proficiency check, required of all Mohawk pilots. He is being checked out by Walter W. Bailey, Link operator and ground instructor, on July 17, 1956.
Courtesy Democrat and Chronicle archives

BOTTOM LEFT: A subway car heads down the tracks to pass under the Culver bridge in 1956. The subway service was in its last days on June 21, 1956, and youngsters take a moment to wave goodbye.
Courtesy Democrat and Chronicle archives

BELOW: The first three girders of the Troup Street Bridge to be put in place across water are loaded onto a barge. A load of braces to go between the girders is lowered by crane to a spot marked by the crew July 20, 1954. *Courtesy Local History Division, Central Library of Rochester and Monroe County*

ABOVE: Mayor Peter Barry cuts a cake topped by a model of Capital Airlines' turbine-powered Viscount at a ceremony marking the beginning of turbo-prop plane service to Rochester. Stewardesses Tony Fry, left, and Nancy Hazelette hold the cake as Harvest Queen Marilyn Kita waits to take a piece up the ramp to the pilot on July 19, 1956. *Courtesy Local History Division, Central Library of Rochester and Monroe County*

TOP LEFT: George O'Donnell tries the door of the subway entrance only to find it locked on July 11, 1956. The subway notice sign reads "To our patrons: On Sunday, June 30, subway passenger service will be operated for the last time. May we express our deep appreciation for your patronage over the years." *Courtesy Local History Division, Central Library of Rochester and Monroe County*

BOTTOM LEFT: This Rochester Transit Corp. veteran subway freight crew would be retained after June 30, 1956. The foursome had a combined service of 151 years as of April 1956, in the trolley operation. From left are Abraham DeHond, Jim Erskine, Bill Boyle and Abraham Leenhouts. *Courtesy Democrat and Chronicle archives*

FAR LEFT: Passenger service on Rochester's subway would be a thing of the past after June 30, 1956, so boarding the trolley for their first, and last, ride are Mr. and Mrs. Robert Hoppe of Irondequoit, and their children, Robert, 9, Christina, 8, Richard, 5, and Paul, 3. Aiding them is motorman Stanley Lewicki. Many other families also took the ride on the line for the last time the week earlier.
Courtesy Democrat and Chronicle archives

ABOVE: Red Cap Claude Butler, left, shown in March 1958 with Alfred Perlman, president of the New York Central Railroad. Perlman had issued an order discontinuing the Red Cap service. *Courtesy Local History Division, Central Library of Rochester and Monroe County*

RIGHT: Elevated parking garage in downtown Rochester, 1960. This photo won a McMaster award that year. *Courtesy Casper Paprocki*

BELOW: By the summer of 1969 pedestrians were able to walk across the Genesee River pedestrian bridge, seen here under construction in January 1969. *Courtesy Democrat and Chronicle archives*

LEFT: Conductor Otto Dietterie helps Mrs. Walter Streb climb aboard the last passenger train to run on the Falls branch of the New York Central Railroad. Mrs. Streb got off at Lockport on Nov. 26, 1957. *Courtesy Local History Division, Central Library of Rochester and Monroe County*

FAR LEFT: John Lombardo, left, and Ray Miller, Rochester Transit Corp. bus drivers, drop their ballots in a box at State Street barns on a compromise wage-hour proposal. Some 900 bus and subway workers voted on a formula to settle the dispute with the company on Oct. 29, 1957. *Courtesy Democrat and Chronicle archives*

BOTTOM LEFT: Small merchant marchers move through East Main Street on their way to City Hall and a conference with Mayor Peter Barry to protest a bus strike on Dec. 1, 1961. They claimed the Christmas shopping season was suffering because of the strike. *Courtesy Democrat and Chronicle archives*

BELOW: View of the Rochester-Monroe County Airport, 1963. The expansion program that year included more convenient boarding facilities for passengers, a longer runway, a larger terminal building, and other facilities to service increasing business. *Courtesy Local History Division, Central Library of Rochester and Monroe County*

Commerce & Industry

The war effort defined Rochester industry through the mid-1940s. Eastman Kodak Co., Gleason Works, Bausch & Lomb, Rochester Products and Odenbach Shipbuilding Co., were in round-the-clock production. As 29,000 Rochester-area men went off to war, jobs became available to thousands of women and minority members who had been discriminated against during the Depression.

Rochester moved from a wartime to a peacetime economy. Returning veterans set off a housing boom. In a decade, the farmland that encircled Rochester was ringing with the sounds of hammers on nails as homes were built at a breakneck pace. The GI Bill allowed more people than ever to go to college.

With education and money in their pockets, Rochesterians began buying goods not available previously. This led to corporate expansion and more job opportunities. Rochester's mix of an educated work force and a spirit of innovation saw the city grow as a technological center. The Haloid Co. became Xerox Corp. and lent its name to a whole new industry.

As consumers became more sophisticated, Rochester merchants responded. From Robert Wegman converting his grocery stores to a self-serve format in 1949 to the construction of Midtown Plaza, the nation's first downtown indoor mall in 1962, Rochester continued to show its boomtown spirit as a commercial power.

LEFT: Dennis Moore, Joe Ryan and John Boylin pose in front of a group of Chevys outside the Morinelli's Richfield Gas Station, 1957. The station was located on the corner of Indiana Street and Atlantic Avenue. *Courtesy Joe Ryan*

ABOVE: James Lunny, assistant to official U.S. Weather Observer Emil A. P. Raab, is shown checking a rain recorder at The Rochester Municipal Airport on July 17, 1945. The apparatus is known as the recording rain gauge but also measures snow and sleet. *Courtesy Local History Division, Central Library of Rochester and Monroe County*

TOP RIGHT: George H. Hawks, president of Rochester Trust and Safe Deposit Company, seated, talks with Raymond N. Ball, the president of Lincoln Alliance Bank and Trust Co., about the proposed merger of their institutions on May 10, 1945. *Courtesy Local History Division, Central Library of Rochester and Monroe County*

BOTTOM RIGHT: Harlow "Jim" Power, standing in front of the old Bausch & Lomb Optical Co. building on St. Paul Street shortly after arriving home from World War II in 1945. His father, Marceau Power, brother Chet Power and sister Jane Power Reisig were employed by Bausch & Lomb. *Courtesy Sharon DiFelice*

FAR RIGHT: Bart Molinari, television engineer, explains the workings of the $55,000 monitor control board to Irene Gedney at the "wired" demonstration of television on April 12, 1940. *Courtesy Democrat and Chronicle archives*

ABOVE: All divisions in modern warfare do not march at the front. Columns and columns of loaded coal cars endlessly pull to the shores of Lake Ontario for transportation to Canada through Rochester and Sodus Point on May 21, 1940. Pennsylvania Railroad officials reported they were carrying double the coal cargoes of normal years, and Baltimore and Ohio officials reported "considerable increases." Consignments were guarded carefully and the photographer had to push through an entanglement of red tape just to get the shot.
Courtesy Democrat and Chronicle Archives

BELOW: Critic's restaurant at night on North Clinton Avenue North with Margaret Lakebury and Magdeline Perry in 1944.
Courtesy Audrey Paprocki

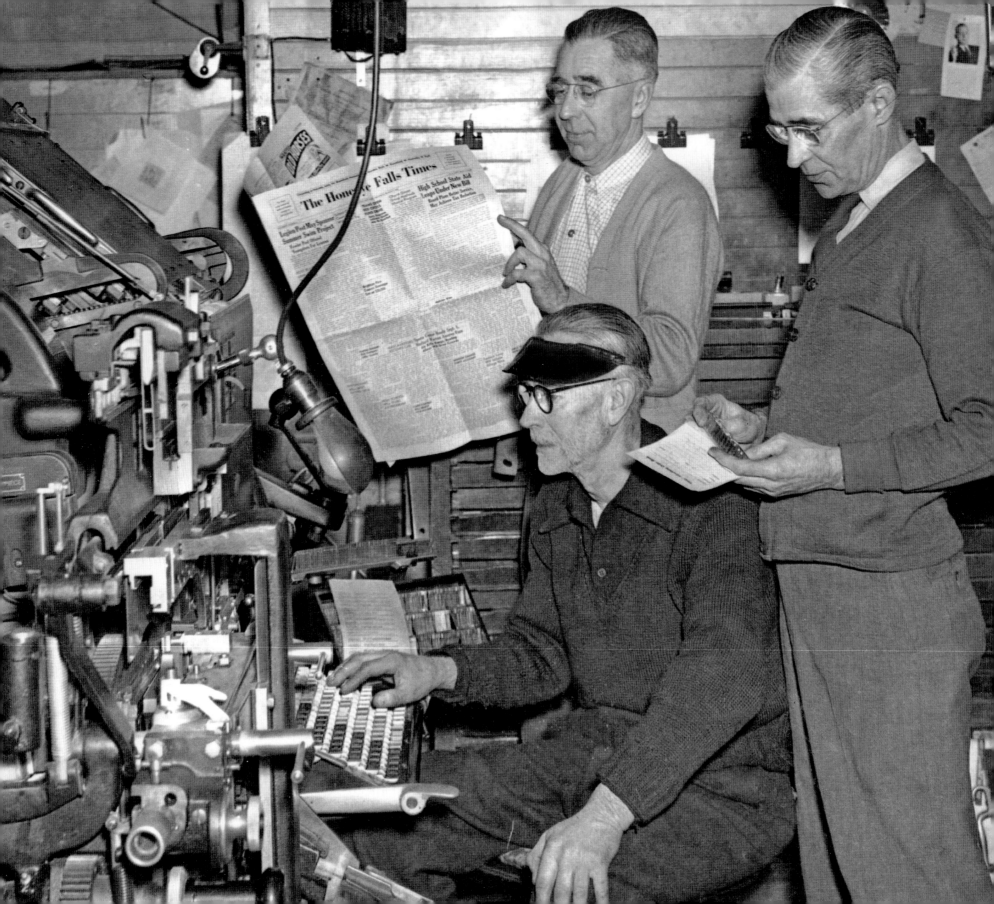

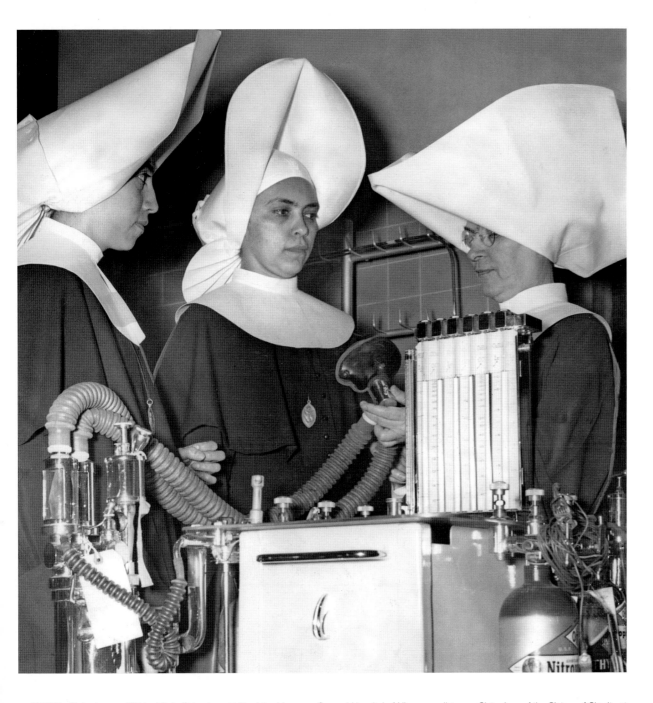

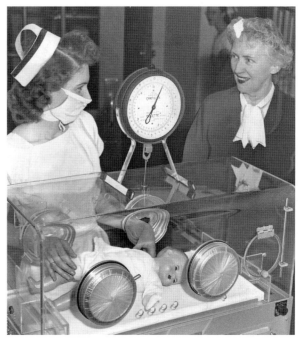

ABOVE: Nurse Mary Lou Cloonan practices handling a doll in the new Isolette presented to General Hospital by its Twig Organization on March 12, 1950. Mrs. Thomas J. Hargrave, right, made the presentation. The Isolette, for care of premature and very ill infants, kept temperature and humidity constant and supplied pure, filtered air that could be enriched with oxygen. The Twig Organization paid $700 for the device. *Courtesy Local History Division, Central Library of Rochester and Monroe County*

BELOW: Joseph R. Wilson and his son, Joseph C., chairman of the board and president, respectively, of Haloid Co., 1948.
Courtesy Democrat and Chronicle archives

ABOVE: Sister Inez and Sister Maria Salvador, at left, of the Managua General Hospital of Nicaragua, listen as Sister Inez of the Sisters of Charity at St. Mary's Hospital explains new hospital equipment. The visitors studied American techniques, July 28, 1947.
Courtesy Local History Division, Central Library of Rochester and Monroe County

OPPOSITE: The *Honeoye Falls Times* was owned by three brothers in 1948. Seated is Harry J. O'Brien. Holding a copy of the paper is McKendree O'Brien and next to him stands William O'Brien, examining lead type, which had already been set. It was called a "slug."
Courtesy Democrat and Chronicle archives

ABOVE: Atlantic Food Market at 944 Atlantic Ave., at the corner of Minnesota Street, circa 1947. The store was owned and operated by Sam and Marge Catone. *Courtesy David Catone*

TOP RIGHT: Dial telephones became a reality for part of Rochester on Aug. 27, 1948. Shown inspecting the new mechanism at work are, from left, John W. Morrison, administrator; Ellery Stone, William Hatton, director of engineering, Federal Telephone and Radio Corp.; and L.J. Denney, director of manufacturing, Federal Telephone and Radio Corp. *Courtesy Democrat and Chronicle archives*

BOTTOM RIGHT: Interested visitors to The *Democrat and Chronicle's* new classified advertising telephone room on Jan. 20, 1948, were Kenneth Ward, left, and Earle Blanchard, classified advertising managers of the *Hartford Courant* and *Schenectady Gazette*, respectively. They watch "Miss Want Ad" at work. *Courtesy Democrat and Chronicle archives*

FAR BOTTOM RIGHT: Miss Ruth Commons, Genesee Exchange operator, demonstrates how a dial call to a non-dial exchange would be handled on June 2, 1949. Numbers on an oblong board in front of the operator light up when a call comes in and the operator plugs in the corresponding party. *Courtesy Democrat and Chronicle archives*

ABOVE: Merritt Torrey, an Eastman Theatre electrician, is at the switch board nerve center controlling the theater lights June 18, 1950. *Courtesy Democrat and Chronicle archives*

TOP LEFT: Jack Van Rue, Bob Clerks and other sales people pose at McGuire Furniture Shop during the post-World War II era, Palmyra, 1947. *Courtesy Adrienne Perrin*

BOTTOM LEFT: An aerial view showing progress on the Mount Morris Dam construction project Aug. 24, 1950. Officials in charge were awaiting a ruling on whether or not work would continue under a "freeze" of non-essential projects. More than half-finished here, the dam had already taken shape with more than 200,000 cubic yards of concrete to complete the foundation. *Courtesy Democrat and Chronicle archives*

FAR BOTTOM LEFT: Springut's Luncheonette on the corner of Clinton and Central avenues, across from the railroad station, circa 1950. It was owned and operated by Max and Barbara Springut.
Courtesy Jeffrey Springut

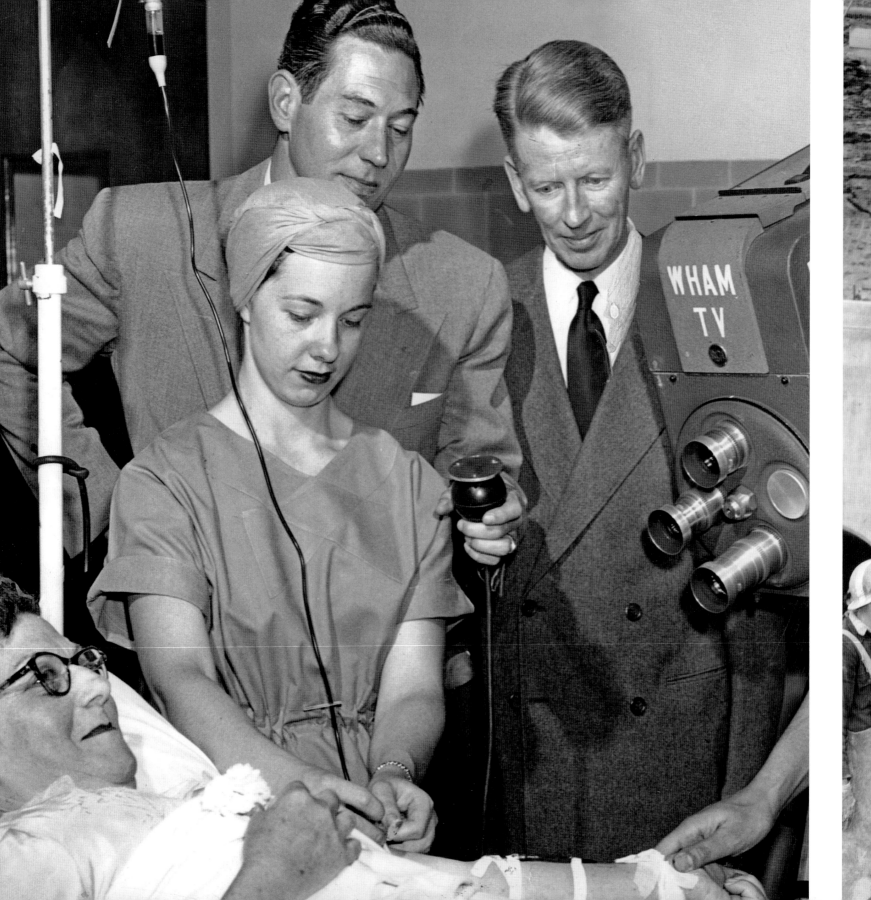

ABOVE: Kimball Tower Factory (later City Hall Annex) about to be demolished to clear the way for the Community War Memorial, circa 1950. Note the statue of Mercury atop the smokestack. It was later moved across Broad Street to it's current location. *Courtesy Local History Division, Central Library of Rochester and Monroe County*

LEFT: Workers dump the last bucket of concrete at the Mount Morris Dam construction site in October 1951. *Courtesy Democrat and Chronicle archives*

OPPOSITE: Rebecca Simons, a patient at the Genesee Hospital, is shown being given a blood transfusion, administered by Dr. Edward Mulligan, which was televised on June 12, 1952. The nurse in the photo is Lorraine Teetsel. Behind her, from left, are Ross Weller, WHAM-TV announcer, and Lawrence Bradley, hospital administrator. *Courtesy Democrat and Chronicle archives*

BELOW: The original location of O'Loughlin's Restaurant, photographed Feb. 19, 1952. The address of the original building was 5370 St. Paul Blvd. in Irondequoit. *Courtesy Debra Klee*

ABOVE: Monroe County Sheriff Albert Skinner leans from his car to make the first deposit at the drive-in teller's window of the new Dewey-Stone branch of Lincoln Rochester Trust Co. at 2900 Dewey Ave. Looking on are John W. Remington, right, bank president, and Raymond N. Ball, board chairman. Greece Supervisor Gordon A. Howe cut the ribbon to open the bank. The branch, formerly at 2885 Dewey, opened on Nov. 22, 1954.
Courtesy Local History Division, Central Library of Rochester and Monroe County

TOP RIGHT: With assurance that the proposed Northside Hospital would become a reality as a result of a sizable Kodak gift, Allen Macomber, co-chairman of the building committee; Elliott Gumaer, president of the hospital fund; and Carey H. Brown, co-chairman of the building committee, inspect the site where construction soon began, June 14, 1953. *Courtesy Local History Division, Central Library of Rochester and Monroe County*

BOTTOM RIGHT: A patient at Rochester State Hospital undergoes a treatment called electric shock therapy, with Dr. Anthony Graffeo, far right, holding a pair of electrodes over the patient's head. A four-person team holds the patient so that he will not injure himself May 21, 1952. *Courtesy Local History Division, Central Library of Rochester and Monroe County*

BELOW: People begin to flock to the Rochester General Hospital for care as a result of the hospitalization insurance on Jan. 19, 1955. *Courtesy Local History Division, Central Library of Rochester and Monroe County*

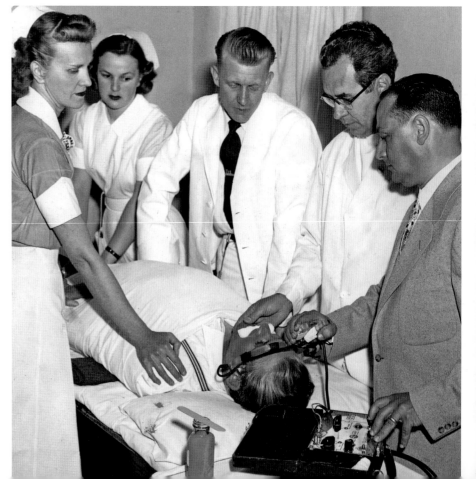

ABOVE: The Weber family house, built at the turn of the 20th century, has one of the first neon signs, advertising Weber's Milk in 1952. The dairy was behind the house. *Courtesy Judith W. Shaw*

BELOW: Preston Jacobs of Avon pushes a painting machine to mark off the stalls at the new Genesee Valley Regional Market at East Henrietta and Jefferson roads in Henrietta on July 23, 1956. *Courtesy Democrat and Chronicle archives*

ABOVE: Another member of the fraternity of Rochester auto agencies is Packard Rochester Inc. at 675 E. Main St. The grand opening was scheduled for December 1952. *Courtesy Democrat and Chronicle archives*

BELOW: The Savoy Hotel, photographed in 1952. Originally known as the Waverly, the building was scheduled to be torn down by the summer of 1953 to make way for the first section of the Inner Loop. *Courtesy Democrat and Chronicle archives*

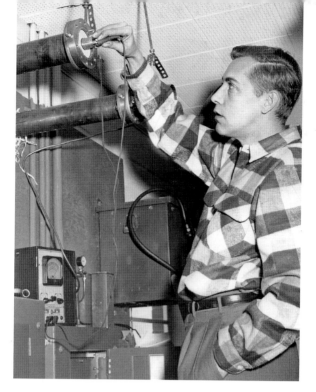

ABOVE: Meisenzahl Dairy in 1956, is best known for its home-delivery of milk and dairy products from the 1930s through the 1970s. By the 1960s, with 14 trucks on 28 routes covering most of Monroe County, it became the region's largest independent dairy. In 1955, the family added homemade ice cream to their menu of dairy products. Their ice cream's reputation grew rapidly area-wide, and attracted thousands every weekend to their new dairy store built in 1957. By the late 1960s, approximately 625 gallons of ice cream was served on weekends. *Courtesy Richard Meisenzahl*

TOP MIDDLE: Francis Sherwood, assistant chief engineer of WHEC-TV, tests the lead-in of the coaxial cable Jan. 15, 1954.
Courtesy Democrat and Chronicle archives

TOP LEFT: The heart of the new microwave relay station was this collection of electronic gadgets for picking up and passing along TV programs. Vertical panels, known as "bays," could each handle one video transmission moving in a single direction, Jan. 17, 1953.
Courtesy Democrat and Chronicle archives

BOTTOM LEFT: In preparation for final repairs on the ceiling of the the Eastman Theatre, workers erect a scaffold, lower right, on March 5, 1955. The scaffold, made from special tubing, took three weeks to put up. The scaffold at left, was used in tests of ceiling, and is not part of structure at lower right. Scaffolding was also built around the huge chandelier. *Courtesy Democrat and Chronicle archives*

OPPOSITE: The WHAM television station broadcasts from a class-room in February 1953. *Courtesy Democrat and Chronicle archives*

TOP LEFT: Cleaning and polishing up the interior of the newly opened Northside Division of the Rochester General Hospital are these women from Kindling Twig, whose members lived in the hospital area, Aug. 2, 1956. Volunteers shining up sterilizing equipment under the eye of executive housekeeper Helen Smith, left, are Mrs. Sidney Roy Cable, center and Mrs. Carroll McBride. *Courtesy Local History Division, Central Library of Rochester and Monroe County*

BELOW: Curt Gerling book signing at the Book Depot, Sibley and Co., 1957. *Courtesy Bill Gerling*

ABOVE: Tools for patients at Rochester State Hospital are shown by George E. Wemett, occupational therapy instructor, to Mrs. Ed K. Bo, a visitor on tour, April 28, 1959.
Courtesy Local History Division, Central Library of Rochester and Monroe County

OPPOSITE: Spaghetti sauce is raised to a high temperature at the Ragu plant at 1680 Lyell Ave. as Ralph Cantisano and brother Frank operate modern equipment Feb. 3, 1957. The sauce was made from a recipe brought from Italy. Founded in 1937 by the Cantisano family, Ragú became the best selling pasta sauce in the United States. *Courtesy Democrat and Chronicle Archives*

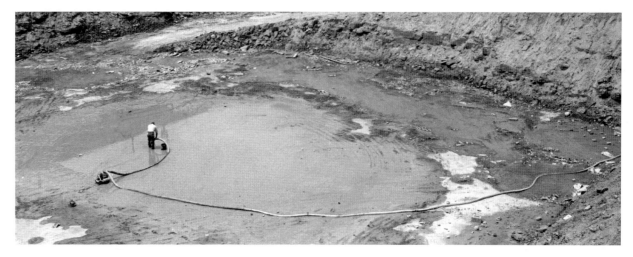

ABOVE: A lone worker pumps water out of a giant pit in downtown Rochester on July 25, 1959. Tons of dirt were hauled from this area, which would become the multi-million-dollar Midtown Plaza, America's first indoor shopping center. *Courtesy Democrat and Chronicle archives*

TOP LEFT: Officials watch a demonstration of the power lift in the Grocers Co-op warehouse, on its opening day, July 11, 1959, at Genesee Valley Regional Market. From left are Bernard Fox, assistant warehouse manager; Joseph King, market administrator; Raymond J. Tierney, in charge of the building; John DeWolf, warehouse manager and William Stoddart, who is operating the lift truck. *Courtesy Democrat and Chronicle archives*

TOP RIGHT: Perini Construction Corp. digs some more earth from the giant Midtown Plaza hole in downtown Rochester on July 22, 1959. The contractors, who built the first half of the Plaza garage, said they would have to dig for several weeks before they could start construction. *Courtesy Democrat and Chronicle archives*

LEFT: Ground-breaking of the Civic Center in January 1958. Mayor Peter Barry is shown speaking from the stage. *Courtesy Local History Division, Central Library of Rochester and Monroe County*

ABOVE: Hanging the sign of the Gannett Newspapers *Times-Union* in Rochester, 1959. The sign was a revolving sign with *Democrat and Chronicle* on one side and *Times-Union* on the other. The large sign, which weighs 2 tons and is three stories high, is erected by crane in Times Square in April 1959. The building, formerly The Times-Union Building, became occupied by two Gannett newspapers.
Courtesy Local History Division, Central Library of Rochester and Monroe County

ABOVE: Xerox copiers at the Xerox building in 1960. *Courtesy Democrat and Chronicle archives*

LEFT: Kramer's Restaurant, located at 216 E. Main St., won second place in the Better Downtown Contest, 1960. *Courtesy Democrat and Chronicle archives*

BELOW: No more "Number, please." At 2:01 a.m. these huge switchboards at the old Hillside central office would stop humming and lights would go out. The team of 87 female operators who had served the exchange around the clock would never return to these chairs, and most were trained for other positions with Rochester Telephone. The switchboards were replaced by Chapel 3 at the Gilbert 4 dial office, December 1961.
Courtesy Democrat and Chronicle archives

ABOVE: A cameraman zeroes in on a studio interview by Tom Decker, right, in the newly remodeled WROC-TV facilities on Apr. 2, 1962. *Courtesy Democrat and Chronicle archives*

TOP RIGHT: This block was scheduled to be razed for the new Xerox building complex on July 16, 1963. The view is across South Clinton Avenue. *Courtesy Democrat and Chronicle archives*

BOTTOM RIGHT: Loew's Theater becomes dark after 37 years as stagehand Dominic Zacaria hauls on rope that closed the curtain for the last time just before midnight on Oct. 4, 1964. Opened as an ornate showpiece of theater architecture and interior decor, the motion picture house at South Clinton Avenue and Court Street was scheduled to be demolished to provide a site for the new Xerox Corp. complex. *Courtesy Democrat and Chronicle archives*

FAR RIGHT: Nicholas DiFilippe, worker at L.C. Forman Co. in Pittsford, scoops a large strainer-full of pickles from a huge brine vat. From here, pickles start on their way to the cleaner, slicer and packager in 1964. *Courtesy Democrat and Chronicle archives*

ABOVE: Charles Horan of the U.S. Housing and Home Finance Agency attacks a building with a sledgehammer, signaling the start of demolition for the Genesee Crossroads project in April 1965. The appreciative audience includes Councilman William J. Malley, center, and Mayor Frank T. Lamb, in helmet, at right.
Courtesy Democrat and Chronicle archives

RIGHT: This 320-foot crane was put into operation on May 3, 1966, at Midtown, where Xerox's new skyscraper was under construction. The crane was used to hoist concrete into the structure.
Courtesy Democrat and Chronicle archives

TOP RIGHT: A crowd gathers to view the newly unveiled Clock of the Nations in Rochester's Midtown Plaza in June 1962. The clock featured scenes from 12 countries and was 28 feet high.
Courtesy Democrat and Chronicle archives

FAR RIGHT: The one-acre Midtown Plaza Mall, which opened its doors on April 10, 1962. In the center of the mall is the 28-foot-high "Clock of the Nations." To the right is a 20-foot living areca palm tree. From this completely covered and air-conditioned mall area, shoppers had access to more than 1 million square feet of retail space, including the McCurdy store and the B. Forman store, co-sponsors of the Midtown project. Photo taken May 20, 1964.
Courtesy Democrat and Chronicle archives

ABOVE: Harper Method Beauty Salon at 5 St. Paul, Room 531, in the Burke Building, 1966.
Courtesy Local History Division, Central Library of Rochester and Monroe County

BELOW: Olga Matigiw polishes the crystal chandelier at the Eastman Theatre on Sept. 6, 1968.
Courtesy Democrat and Chronicle archives

ABOVE: Xerox Square, the nearly-completed new Rochester headquarters of Xerox Corp., attained full occupancy on Aug. 5, 1968, when the company's Latin American operations group moved into the annex building (low structure in left, foreground). Most of the corporate staff activities were housed in the 440-foot, 30-story building at rear. White structure in center foreground is an auditorium and exhibit hall. Barely visible behind it is a sunken ice skating rink. Fully-enclosed, weather-conditioned, pedestrian bridges interconnect the three buildings with one another and with Midtown Plaza, across the street, a combined indoor shopping center, office building and penthouse hotel-restaurant. *Courtesy Democrat and Chronicle archives*

Schools & Education

With the outbreak of World War II, Rochester's schools faced problems. Enrollment of older students was dropping as they sought jobs or military service. Enrollment of younger students was growing as their mothers went to work.

Fueled by the baby boom, the 1950s saw primary and secondary school enrollment levels soar, and schools began to burst at their seams. Greece Olympia and the new East High School were shining examples of construction that brought much-needed classroom space, along with improvements to class size and teacher-pupil ratio, to area schools.

As if that wasn't enough, *Sputnik* and the space race with Russia added pressure to all American schools to add new technologies and educational techniques. And Rochester responded in characteristic "can-do" fashion.

As the wave of baby boomers grew up, colleges in the Rochester area grew with them. The University of Rochester grew dramatically in the 10 years after World War II, doubling its faculty and adding to its River Campus. The Mechanics Institute became Rochester Institute of Technology in 1947. RIT moved its campus from downtown to a new site in Henrietta in 1968.

By 1969, the nine colleges and universities located in Monroe County meant education was well on its way to becoming Rochester's second biggest industry.

LEFT: Students from the class of 1940, School No. 52.
Courtesy Donald Murrell

ABOVE: Miss De Lay's class from Ruben A. Drake School, June 1945. Identified is Bill Peck Jr., in the front row, on the far right end.
Courtesy Debra Klee

TOP: Flag-raising ceremonies are held in conjunction with the start of the fall term at Franklin High School on Sept. 5, 1947. Participating students included standardbearer David Wallace and co-guardians of the flag Tobinette Holtz and Joyce Frankel. The ritual began in the early years of World War II and continued as a peacetime practice.
Courtesy Local History Division, Central Library of Rochester and Monroe County

LEFT: Four pupils of Rochester Public School No. 6 sit at the entrance of their school, which would soon close its doors on June 2, 1944.
Courtesy Local History Division, Central Library of Rochester and Monroe County

OPPOSITE: The sixth-grade class at Reuben A. Dake Elementary School, Irondequoit in 1945. In the fourth row, far right, is Dick Peck.
Courtesy Karen Ogle and Janet Chippero

ABOVE: Kaelber Class at Salem Church in downtown Rochester, 1950. Identified in the front row, third from left, are Wilbur Peck Sr. and in the front row, at the right end, is Carl Nolte. *Courtesy Debra Klee*

BELOW: Classroom from No. 8 School, 1948. *Courtesy Ken and Mary Feicht*

ABOVE: Irondequoit High School football team ready to play in the fall of 1950. Number 46 in the front row is Dick Peck. *Courtesy Karen Ogle and Janet Chippero*

BELOW: Winners of the 1949-1950 McCurdy Music School scholarships smile at Gordon W. McCurdy, vice president of McCurdy & Co. In front row, from left, are McCurdy, Donald Mead, and Ellen Hettel. Back row, Harry Mesina Jr., Richard Dennison, Helen Bilhorn, and Martha Walker. They were formally presented with the awards at Rochester Radio City. *Courtesy Local History Division, Central Library of Rochester and Monroe County*

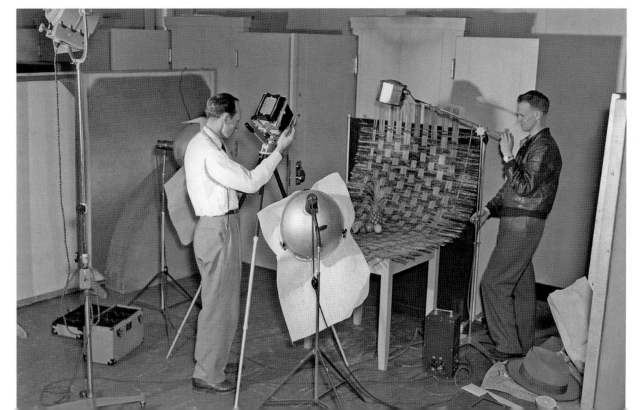

ABOVE: Workers update a billboard on the site of Rochester Institute of Technology's new 1,300-acre campus in Henrietta, Sept. 18, 1963. RIT made the decision to move from their downtown campus in 1961, and ground was broken for the massive project in 1964. The school moved in 1968, dedicating the new campus in October of that year.
Courtesy Democrat and Chronicle archives

LEFT: Rochester Institute of Technology students, Willis Sanders, left and Earl Reiber-Mohn, an exchange student from Norway, work in a photo studio in the George H. Clark building on RIT's downtown campus. Heralded as the best photography program and equipment in the world, these photo students were trying to solve an experimental photographic problem as a class assignment, June 9, 1947.
Courtesy Democrat and Chronicle archives

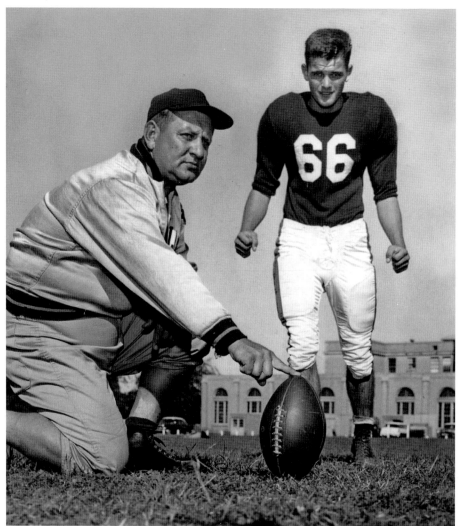

ABOVE: Brighton High School football coach Herb Carlberg checks probable starting lineups for a LeRoy game with co-captains Bob Savage, left, and Tim Burgess on Sept. 6, 1957. Savage played left tackle and Burgess left guard. *Courtesy Local History Division, Central Library of Rochester and Monroe County*

TOP RIGHT: Joe Repko, coach, and Ron Chatterton, kicking, from Aquinas Institute during warm-ups on the field, September 1957. *Courtesy Local History Division, Central Library of Rochester and Monroe County*

BOTTOM RIGHT: Pictured, from left, are Helen Hart, Colleen Liese, Tom Hauser; prom king, Pat Lins; prom queen, the Junior Class Queen and King who are unidentified, Joan Grasick and Mary Ann Geraci at the Junior/Senior Prom at Churchville-Chili High School in 1954. *Courtesy Helen Bischoping & Noreen Crouse*

ABOVE: Old East High School greets students on Sept. 3, 1958, for its 56th school year. Officials were studying what to do with the Alexander Street building after the new East High School opened in 1959.
Courtesy Democrat and Chronicle archives

TOP LEFT: The new East High School takes shape between East Main Street, right, and Atlantic Avenue, upper left. The $10.8 million project included an auditorium, cafeteria, shop wing and gymnasium and pool. Other wings contain classrooms, student center and library, Sept. 3, 1958.
Courtesy Democrat and Chronicle archives

BOTTOM LEFT: The old Elmgrove School at 451 Elmgrove Rd. Greece, a two-classroom midget was sold for $10,400. About 70 builders and spectators, mostly spectators, attended the auction in March 1959.
Courtesy Democrat and Chronicle archives

ABOVE: Nathaniel Hawthorne School No. 25, a grammar school, in 1968. *Courtesy Ken and Mary Feicht*

TOP: Students come and go from the new Olympia High School in Greece in 1959. *Courtesy Democrat and Chronicle archives*

TOP RIGHT: School No. 35 fourth-graders watch the television screen as Geraldine McMullen narrates the first in a series of educational television programs on Jan. 7, 1959. *Courtesy Democrat and Chronicle archives*

BOTTOM RIGHT: The biggest and newest educational plant in the city, at that time, was Rochester's East High School, costing $12 million and dedicated on May 1, 1960. *Courtesy Democrat and Chronicle archives*

ABOVE: The John Marshall High School boys basketball team from the 1951-1952 season. From left are Coach Bushnell, K. Rhoads, D. Donavan, D. Simpson, D. Bentley, M. Korol, L. DeFrancesco, D. Evgenides, A. Tirassi, R. Pica, B. Mears, and D. Holledel. *Courtesy M. Yvonne Holman Hamilton*

TOP: The John Marshall High School baseball team from the 1951-1952 season. Identified in the front row, from left, are R. Morrison, E. DeRyke, D. McKnight, D. Simpson, F. Raforth and K. Rhoades. In the back row, from left, are R. Harter, L. DeFrancesco, R. Pica, Coach Bushnell, N. Trevor, D. Bentley and E. Tripp. *Courtesy M. Yvonne Holman Hamilton*

TOP LEFT: James E. Sutherland, a Charlotte High School senior, stands in front of his school's symbol, the lighthouse behind Holy Cross Church on Lake Avenue in March 1966. In 1965, hearing rumors that the old lighthouse was to be torn down, the editor of the Charlotte High School newspaper, *The Pilot*, wrote an editorial urging the community to save the landmark. The community responded, and the structure was saved. *Courtesy Democrat and Chronicle archives*

BOTTOM LEFT: Robert Reeve, seated at the desk under the lights in the background, gives the first lesson over East High School's closed-circuit TV station. Cameraman at left is a student, Ted Papke, on May 7, 1963. *Courtesy Democrat and Chronicle archives*

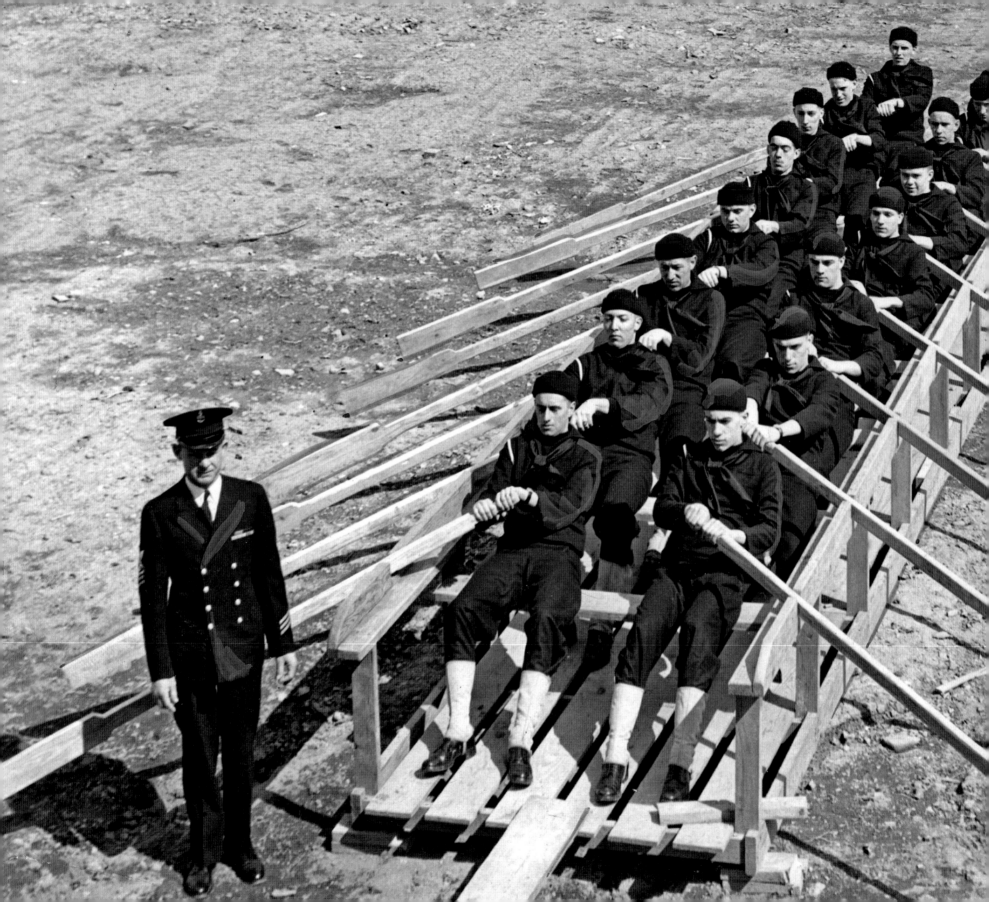

Public Service

Supporting the war effort, whether in uniform or on the home front, was a service that consumed nearly every American – man or woman.

Besides the military, public service took other forms. In 1948, the Greater Rochester Chapter of the American Red Cross began the first civilian blood collection program in the United States and was the first chapter to send blood to servicemen in Korea.

The Cold War brought a whole new dimension to public service. Police officers and firefighters adopted new technologies to make their jobs safer and protect the community from an unseen enemy. Volunteers joined Civil Defense units around the community, conducted "duck and cover" drills in schools and provisioned fallout shelters.

Perhaps the most obvious example of public service in the United States is the commander in chief. Rochester residents turned out by the thousands to attend presidential campaign rallies to catch a glimpse of future presidents Truman, Eisenhower, Kennedy and Nixon. They also took to the streets to mourn the passing of two great public servants, taken down in the service of their country – in November 1963 for John Kennedy and again in April 1968 for Martin Luther King Jr.

LEFT: Sampson Naval Training Station blue-jackets preparing for the icy water of Seneca Lake. Under the watchful eye of Chief Boatswain-Mate George Strobel, recruits are being given preliminary instructions in the fundamentals of rowing. As soon as they mastered pulling an oar, the men were given further instruction on Seneca in one of the 150 whale boats at the station. *Courtesy Local History Division, Central Library of Rochester and Monroe County*

ABOVE: Every day at 1 p.m. during War Week 1942, loudspeakers along Main Street carried the strains of "The Star Spangled Banner" to people in the street. Here at respectful attention, from left, James Farasey, police Sgt. Joe Hauser and John Evans.
Courtesy Local History Division, Central Library of Rochester and Monroe County

LEFT: Sailors on board a U.S. Naval Reserve ship on the Genesee River near Summerville, on Oct. 24, 1940.
Courtesy Local History Division, Central Library of Rochester and Monroe County

OPPOSITE TOP LEFT: New York National Guard members from the 21st Regiment are shown in the target trenches in November 1941. The men are Isadore Cahen, Maurice Cahen, George Stalz and Captain Vince A. Palmer. *Courtesy Local History Division, Central Library of Rochester and Monroe County*

OPPOSITE BOTTOM LEFT: This blue and crimson pennant, symbolic of the new joint Army-Navy production award, is held aloft by Eastman Kodak Co. president Thomas J. Hargrave and a Kodak machinist at the left named Lehle (no first name given), on Aug. 17, 1942. Nearly 20,000 Kodak employees gathered at Red Wing Stadium for the presentation by Brig. Gen. Herman Schull as a reward for Kodak's "skill and steadfastness." *Courtesy Democrat and Chronicle archives*

OPPOSITE TOP RIGHT: Harper Sibley at the Genesee Country Club in January 1941, at a dinner honoring his service to the YMCA. Speakers at the table, from left are Herb Lanedale Jr., Reed Shutt, Henry Shedd, Eugene Bennett, unknown, unknown, Harper Sibley, Louie Faulks, and Edgar Allen Stibbins. Seated at the front table are Shorty Meader, William Briggs, Bob Bunting, Guy Mahley, unknown, Jackson Gallup, and two unknown men. *Courtesy Local History Division, Central Library of Rochester and Monroe County*

OPPOSITE BOTTOM RIGHT: Chief Claude Dunbar, machinist's mate, and William Maki, machinist's mate, below deck on Nov. 18, 1940.
Courtesy Local History Division, Central Library of Rochester and Monroe County

ABOVE: Mrs. Robert McGlashan approaches a tent to place her donation of books for the Victory Book Campaign in January 1942. *Courtesy Local History Division, Central Library of Rochester and Monroe County*

BELOW: Librarians Elizabeth Sutterland, Genesee branch; Rita Sheldon, catalog division, and Carolyn Castle, Brighton branch, sift through books that were donated for the Victory Book Campaign, January 1942.
Courtesy Local History Division, Central Library of Rochester and Monroe County

ABOVE: Women gather around a display that shows the progress of war bonds purchased in an effort to support the military, circa 1942. *Courtesy Local History Division, Central Library of Rochester and Monroe County*

OPPOSITE: The headquarters of the Military Police at Cobbs Hill had all the amenities of home: a piano, books, tables, magazines, davenports, chairs, phonographs, records, and lamps. It all followed a notice in the *Times-Union* a few days prior suggesting contributions to help make the place more homelike. Shown here enjoying themselves are, from left, Pvt. Harry Potter, Pfc. Peter Healion, Pvt. Edward Nigretti, Pfc. Albert Weingarth, Pvt. Albert Papp, and Cpl. Thomas Cannistre on April 29, 1942. *Courtesy Local History Division, Central Library of Rochester and Monroe County*

BELOW: Businessmen, lawyers, laborers — men from all walks of life — answer the fourth draft call, April 25, 1942. In a line that extended from the basement of the Court House down Main Street to Fitzhugh Street, men waited to register with Board 553 in the fourth draft sign-up in three years. Forty-five thousand men, ages 45 to 65, were anticipated to register that day in the county. The age group included men who had sons in the service and some who served in World War I. *Courtesy Local History Division, Central Library of Rochester and Monroe County*

ABOVE: Bill Almy, center, Phil Almy and "Spark" Almy during Bill's time on leave on Gould Street in 1944.
Courtesy Ken and Mary Feicht

TOP RIGHT: For the first time the "V" symbol of the Allied Powers rose from Italian prisoners of war when these cannery workers in Webster cheered the news of Italy's declaration of war on Germany, which broke when they were at work on Oct. 13, 1943. *Courtesy Local History Division, Central Library of Rochester and Monroe County*

BOTTOM RIGHT: With Geneva's Trinity Church filled with Navy trainees, Lt. H. J. Berkowitz, Jewish chaplain at Sampson Naval Training Station, delivers the invocation which opened the special convocation of Hobart and William Smith Colleges in October 1943. The convocation, attended by persons of all faiths, was called to graduate the first V-12 unit of Hobart and to pay tribute to Charles University of Prague, Czechoslovakia. Thirty-seven graduated. *Courtesy Local History Division, Central Library of Rochester and Monroe County*

BELOW: Busy at work at nearby farms and canning plants are these Italian prisoners of war, shown smiling from the back of an Army truck as they pass through Rochester, Sept. 30, 1943.
Courtesy Local History Division, Central Library of Rochester and Monroe County

TOP FAR LEFT: Patricia Hanna, a farmer from Springwater, drives her tractor and load of tomatoes down Rochester's Main Street as part of the Junior Chamber of Commerce Crop Corps drive to recruit aid for farmers and canners in harvesting the tomato crop in the area on Sept. 15, 1944. *Courtesy Local History Division, Central Library of Rochester and Monroe County*

TOP LEFT: First to sign up for a Sixth War Loan bond at the booth of the Blue Star Brigade was Jean Brown of Geneseo, who was escorted by TSgt. Forrest L. Vosler, Livonia, winner of the congressional Medal of Honor. TSgt. Vosler participated in the christening of the "Tokyo Bond," November 1944. *Courtesy Local History Division, Central Library of Rochester and Monroe County*

BOTTOM LEFT: Military Police of the Army and Nazi war prisoners came to Cobbs Hill Park after the barracks were established on the east side of the city. MPs were used for guard duty of important installations and also controlled German prisoners at work, Sept. 15, 1945. *Courtesy Democrat and Chronicle archives*

BELOW: The War Relocation Authority moved Charles Sawabe from his Santa Clara, Calif. home to the Relocation Center in Arizona, where he earned his business administration degree from Armstrong College. He was then moved to Rochester, where he accepted employment with Bourjois Inc., filling outgoing orders. His foreman, Glenn Graham, said of him, "He is a competent worker, learns quickly, and is well-liked by his associates here," December 1944. *Courtesy Local History Division, Central Library of Rochester and Monroe County*

Gli Soleati
Americani ed
Inglesi Sono
in Francia.

ABOVE: An estimated 20,000 people gathered on Main Street for the official opening of Rochester's Victory Loan Drive on Oct. 30, 1945. Ceremonies under blazing lights and banners were preceded by a parade in which military veterans and high school bands participated. *Courtesy Local History Division, Central Library of Rochester and Monroe County*

LEFT: News of the Allied victory in Europe sends young and old alike to their churches to offer prayers in thanks and ask for divine guidance in the war in the Pacific, on May 9, 1945. Entering St. Luke's Church on Fitzhugh Street are Helen Erle, wife of T3c (torpedo) operator Emmanuel Erle in submarine service in the Pacific; and their son, Leslie, 4; and Pfc. August Corona, veteran of two years of service in England, Italy and Africa. *Courtesy Local History Division, Central Library of Rochester and Monroe County*

OPPOSITE: Shown with a sign held by Pfc. Anthony Valente of the Military Police at Cobbs Hill informing them Europe has been invaded, Italian war prisoners express their joy in cheers on June 7, 1944. *Courtesy Local History Division, Central Library of Rochester and Monroe County*

ABOVE: A U.S. Navy ship is docked at the Municipal Dock near Charlotte, circa 1942. *Courtesy Local History Division, Central Library of Rochester and Monroe County*

TOP RIGHT: Crowds gathered quickly around downtown newsstands on Aug. 10, 1945, as the first extra editions carrying banners of Japan's offer to make peace hit the streets. The *Times-Union* cameraman found this cluster of willing readers at Main and Clinton. *Courtesy Local History Division, Central Library of Rochester and Monroe County*

BOTTOM RIGHT: The biggest group of British evacuees to leave for their homes in England, 43 boys and girls who were cared for by employees of the Eastman Kodak Co. during the German blitz are shown before boarding the train for New York on July 11, 1945. *Courtesy Local History Division, Central Library of Rochester and Monroe County*

OPPOSITE LEFT: Rochester joins together in celebration just after 7 p.m. on Aug. 14, 1945, when the news came in that the bloodiest conflict of World War II was at an end. The news was a signal for all motorists to head downtown. *Courtesy Local History Division, Central Library of Rochester and Monroe County*

OPPOSITE TOP: Rochesterians show their excitement on V-J Day, Aug. 14, 1945. *Courtesy Local History Division, Central Library of Rochester and Monroe County*

OPPOSITE BOTTOM: Exerting every effort to answer the flood of calls on the *Democrat and Chronicle* switchboard, operator Jean Bowan helped to keep Rochester posted on the war situation and the Japanese peace proposal on Aug. 13, 1945. *Courtesy Local History Division, Central Library of Rochester and Monroe County*

ABOVE: Captain and Mrs. S.W. Townsend and Brig. Gen. Kenneth C. Townson at the annual Reserve Officers Military Ball at the University Club on Feb. 19, 1949. *Courtesy Local History Division, Central Library of Rochester and Monroe County*

RIGHT: Rochester Fire Chief John A. Slattery had a helping hand when he tried out his newly installed two-way radio in his Fire Bureau automobile. His grandson, 2-year-old Raymond Slattery, did the *"broadcasting"* Feb. 14, 1947. *Courtesy Local History Division, Central Library of Rochester and Monroe County*

BELOW: Coast Guard Warrant Officer Walter Czechanski launches an annual inspection of safety devices on pleasure craft in Lake Ontario waters. He is joined by his son, Thomas, 13, center, and Thomas' chum, Michael Cappon on July 3, 1952. *Courtesy Local History Division, Central Library of Rochester and Monroe County*

ABOVE: A Coast Guard surf boat from the Summerville Station takes off from Sand Point to rescue two men marooned in a cottage on Charles Point in Sodus Bay in May, 1947. The boat later got caught in ice.
Courtesy Local History Division, Central Library of Rochester and Monroe County

LEFT: Dedication ceremony of the Irondequoit Town Hall on May 30, 1951. *Courtesy Democrat and Chronicle archives*

BELOW: Ranking officers salute as they board the U.S. Naval Reserve Rochester unit's ship for a weekend cruise. From left are Lt. j.g. M.H. La Borie, USN, officer-in-charge; Lt. Cmdr. W.J. Sheehan, USNR, skipper of the cruise; Lt. Cmdr. J.P. Powell, USNR; liaison officer, and Cmdr. Peter Barry, USNR, commanding officer of the 3-3 Brigade, Aug. 30, 1947. *Courtesy Local History Division, Central Library of Rochester and Monroe County*

ABOVE: A crowd gathers to hear Dwight D. Eisenhower speak as he passes through Rochester on a campaign stop in 1952.

Courtesy Democrat and Chronicle archives

TOP LEFT: A crowd estimated at 10,000 jammed Clinton Avenue from Central Avenue to the railroad bridge and an adjoining taxi stand to hear President Truman, on the upper deck, make his speech from the stand erected on the station platform. *Courtesy Local History Division, Central Library of Rochester and Monroe County*

BOTTOM LEFT: Irondequoit Patrolmen Terry Malloy, left, and Frank Dovidio are shown with the department's new white police car. Prior to this time, the police cars were black, but switched over to white in January 1963. *Courtesy Democrat and Chronicle archives*

OPPOSITE TOP LEFT: Deputy Fire Chief Walter Adams (pointing), is in charge of the command post set up at Mount Read Boulevard and Lexington Avenue minutes after the "bomb" fell during a Cold War-era civil defense drill. With him are, from left, Albert J. Court, state CD observer; Norman McGovern, CD volunteer; and B. Richard Townsend, state fire chief from Albany, May 8, 1953. *Courtesy Local History Division, Central Library of Rochester and Monroe County*

OPPOSITE BOTTOM LEFT: City officials get a preview look at the latest life-saving apparatus available to firefighters in 1967. It's a $78,990 self-contained aerial pumper platform, known as a "snorkel." Wheeling over Broad Street were, left, snorkel operator, Public Safety Commissioner Mark Tuohey, City Manager Seymour Scher and Mayor Frank T. Lamb. *Courtesy Democrat and Chronicle archives*

OPPOSITE TOP RIGHT: Bull's Head, in theory at least, was the spot where a bomb hit, and therefore it was completely knocked out. Actually, like the rest of the city, it only came to a temporary halt. Clarence Frederick, a Civil Defense auxiliary policeman, brought traffic to a stop at the theoretical Ground Zero. Pedestrians took cover in buildings, May 9, 1953. *Courtesy Local History Division, Central Library of Rochester and Monroe County*

OPPOSITE BOTTOM RIGHT: Deputy Fire Chief Louis Vogt mans the wheel of this fire pumper truck built at the Rochester Police & Fire Academy at a cost of about $15,000 on June 7, 1958. It is the first in the city to be equipped with electric reels for booster lines and a hydraulic governor to control pump pressure. Capt. Ernest Starr, kneeling, examines accessory equipment used on the truck. The pumper was placed into service the following month and was featured in an open house the following day. *Courtesy Local History Division, Central Library of Rochester and Monroe County*

ABOVE: The Rochester city government rested largely in the hands of these people in 1962. From left at the Democratic headquarters are Frank T. Lamb, Henry R. Dutcher Jr., John G. Bittner, Robert E. O'Brien, Henry E. Gillette, William J. Malley, Charles T. Maloy and Mario J. Pirrello. Dutcher headed the transition committee and O'Brien was the county Democratic chairman. This photo was taken on Nov. 10, 1961. *Courtesy Democrat and Chronicle archives*

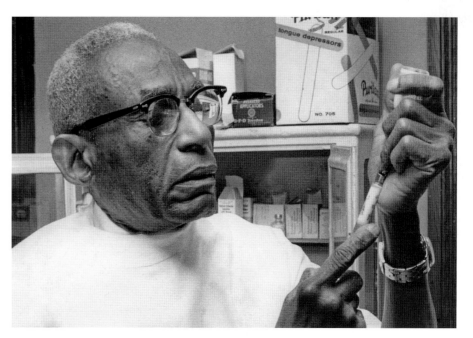

ABOVE: Dr. Anthony Jordan, May 3, 1969. He practiced in the heart of the city of Rochester for 37 years, from his office at 136 Adams St. *Courtesy Democrat and Chronicle archives*

LEFT: A fireman atop an aerial ladder hacks away at the huge icicle on the Pine Alley side of the City Hall on Dec. 27, 1963. The ice posed a threat to passers-by below. *Courtesy Democrat and Chronicle archives*

OPPOSITE: Sen. John F. Kennedy waves to Rochesterians near Water Street as his motorcade moves east along Main Street on Sept. 29, 1960. Detectives are sitting on both sides of the official car and in the car behind. Rochester was among Kennedy's campaign stops for the presidency in 1960. *Courtesy Democrat and Chronicle archives*

ABOVE: Richard Nixon pays a visit to Rochester during his campaign for the presidency in 1960.
Courtesy Democrat and Chronicle archives

LEFT: Extra afternoon editions bring the news of John F. Kennedy's assassination to Rochester on Nov. 22, 1963. *Courtesy Democrat and Chronicle archives.*

FAR LEFT: A mass of Rochesterians jams the Community War Memorial to listen to Vice President Richard M. Nixon, shown on stage at right, deliver his address, on Nov. 1, 1962.
Courtesy Local History Division, Central Library of Rochester and Monroe County

ABOVE: After collapsing at a helicopter crash scene on Clarissa Street, Deputy Police Chief Jensen is carried to an ambulance by city police and sheriff's deputies, during the riots on July 26, 1964.
Courtesy Democrat and Chronicle archives

RIGHT: Guardsmen from the First Howitzer Battalion, 209 Artillery, New York National Guard 209th Artillery prepare to move into the riot zone on July 24, 1964. *Courtesy Democrat and Chronicle archives*

BELOW: These eight Rochester motorcycle officers, led by Sgt. James Neary, right, were part of the increased force of men at work for Memorial Day weekend in 1964. *Courtesy Democrat and Chronicle archives*

OPPOSITE: Members of the Irondequoit Police Department are, from left, Ruth Behnke, Elizabeth Macy, Tillie Schwartz and Constance Di Marco. Police Sgt. Charles Doran is seated in front in 1960.
Courtesy Democrat and Chronicle archives

Community

According to the 1940 U.S. Census, Rochester was the 23rd largest city in the United States, with a population of 324,975.

By 1950, the population of the city had grown to 332,488, but the rest of America was growing too, and Rochester was now only the 32nd largest city in the U.S. The '50s saw movement out of the city of Rochester and the explosive growth of the inner ring of suburbs, Irondequoit, Brighton, Greece, Gates, Chili and Henrietta. This trend mirrored that of cities across the United States. Kodak was Rochester's leading industrial employer and continued to dominate the film and camera industry, but other Rochester companies also boasted significant numbers of technical and manufacturing jobs.

The 1960 census showed a population drop to 318,611 and a drop in rank to 38th. The '60s saw tens of thousands of Rochester children from the post-war baby boom became teenagers and young adults.

The movement away from the conservatism of the '50s eventually resulted in revolutionary ways of thinking and dramatic changes to the cultural fabric of American life. No longer content to be mirrors of the previous generation, young people wanted change. The changes affected all facets of life from education and values to lifestyles and involvement in causes.

LEFT: Kevin Shepard, 21 months old, is given his Sabin anti-polio vaccine. Mrs. Charles Shepard brought Kevin and Charles Jr. to school at 81 Hickory St. as the second round of free vaccinations began on June 20, 1960. Elizabeth Meyer, a public health nurse, gave the next spoonful to Charles. *Courtesy Democrat and Chronicle archives*

ABOVE: Irma and John Wurme, lived at 711 Seward St., circa 1942. John was home on leave from World War II.
Courtesy Lawrence Wurme

TOP RIGHT: A cousins' reunion in front of the family home at 476 Lyell Ave., circa 1943. From left, bottom, is John Lippa and at top are Mary Bianchi, Ursula Lippa, Frances Bianchi, Victor Bianchi, Mary Lippa and Louis Lippa. *Courtesy John Lippa*

MIDDLE RIGHT: Kids help collect scrap metal for a World War II scrap metal drive, November 1942. This spot was purchased by the neighborhood air raid Wardens. It later became The 88 Club, a social club for the men of the neighborhood that was in existence for more than 40 years. From left are Jerry Dunn, Bill Fein, Bud McGrady, George Willis, Robert Willis, Mary Louise Mandia, Dorothy Renner, Barbara Geise and Jack Willis. *Courtesy Gerald Dunn*

BOTTOM RIGHT: Virginia and Dave Howard in front of their home in 1943. *Courtesy Dave Howard*

RIGHT: Frederick Douglass is preserved in a statuesque form in Highland Park. Douglass used to stand near the now-razed New York Central railway station, but his present location is near the site of his house, which was on the Underground Railroad. The statue was moved in the early 1940s. *Courtesy Democrat and Chronicle archives*

ABOVE: Pat and Joyce Mesh in front of the family car on Winterroth Street as Virginia Mesh and Richard look on in 1943.
Courtesy Pat Del Vecchio

TOP: George Murrell in 1944. *Courtesy Donald Murrell*

LEFT: Lois and Angelo Casti with daughter Rosalind Casti Santora, Rochester in 1943. Angelo was on leave from the Navy during World War II. *Courtesy Rosalind Casti Santora*

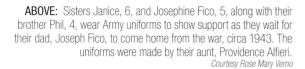

ABOVE: Sisters Janice, 6, and Josephine Fico, 5, along with their brother Phil, 4, wear Army uniforms to show support as they wait for their dad, Joseph Fico, to come home from the war, circa 1943. The uniforms were made by their aunt, Providence Alfieri.
Courtesy Rose Mary Verno

TOP: Doris Von Buren, 6, models a hula skirt, wrist pom-pons and lei in front of the No. 22 school on Leo Street, 1944. The outfit was sent to her by her uncle, Franklin Von Buren, while he was stationed in Maui, Hawaii, for four years during World War II.
Courtesy Cynthia Howk

TOP RIGHT: Dewey and Marion Flowerday, on left, and Ruby and John Selg, on right, catch up while Dewey is home on leave from World War II. *Courtesy Diane Drysdale*

BOTTOM RIGHT: Lyman Lawrence, from Saranac Lake, and his wife, Jane Castlano Lawrence, met on a blind date at the Genesee Hospital School of Nursing in 1941. Jane was from Clyde, and they had two sons, who reside in Rochester. This photo was taken in 1945.
Courtesy Richard Lawrence

ABOVE: Tonia Wojnowski, 7, sees her reflection in the mirror while she brushes her hair in Charlotte in 1946. *Courtesy Reyton Wojnowski*

BELOW: Wedding photograph of Robert and Geraldine Utter in August 1945. In the back row, from left, are Chester Power, June Utter, Marceau Power (father of the bride), Geraldine Utter, Robert Utter, Richard Utter, Jane Reisig and an unidentified usher. In the front row, from left are Louise Binder, Veronica Maslanke, Beverly Power, Tom Collins, Cunice Collins and Louise (last name unknown). *Courtesy Sharon DiFelice*

ABOVE: "Maryann," the host of the children's program *Just for Fun*, hosted by WHEC radio station, 1947. *Courtesy Democrat and Chronicle archives*

BELOW: Frances Gartland relaxes on a 1940 convertible, circa 1947. *Courtesy Edward Gartland*

ABOVE: Just about a month before opening, this structure, The Barn, was a youth center sponsored by The Gannett Newspapers. From left, Donald Woodruff, Virginia Hafner, and Dorothy Ralston, West High seniors, are inspecting the construction at the site in Fair Park on March 30, 1947. *Courtesy Local History Division, Central Library of Rochester and Monroe County*

TOP RIGHT: L. J. M. Daguerre invented the first photographic process, the daguerreotype, in 1839. Eastman House curator Beaumont Newall holds up a camera made that year. It bears the seal with Daguerre's signature. In the background are some of the many old cameras that made up the Eastman House Museum's collection and provided a rare treat for visitors in 1948. *Courtesy Democrat and Chronicle archives*

BOTTOM RIGHT: Books were closed on the Grand Army of the Republic, Department of New York, in ceremonies at Highland Park on June 12, 1948, as thousands paid tribute to comrade James A. Hard, 106-year-old Union veteran. From left are Mrs. Carl E. Eksten, granddaughter of Hard, who is seated; Mayor Samuel Dicker, presenting city certificate to Hard; May Hughes, Rochester, past national president of the Women's Relief Corps, and Emma Swift, head of the history division of Rochester Public Library, who is holding the record book of the GAR, which was turned over to the library by Hard on June 12, 1948. *Courtesy Democrat and Chronicle archives*

OPPOSITE: Compulsory voting was the topic when Junior Town Meetings returned to WHEC in September 1952. In the center is William Adams, WHEC program director. The debaters, all Marshall High School pupils, are, from left, Daniel Stutzman, Carolyn Moore, Sylvia Ewing and William DuBiel. *Courtesy Democrat and Chronicle archives*

ABOVE: Hairdressers Reg Zornow, Jerry Zornow and an unidentified fellow beautician, along with other hairdressers, Ruby Selg and Marion Flowerday, leave the train station in Rochester in 1952.
Courtesy Diane Drysdale

RIGHT: Judy Pembroke of Pittsford demonstrates use of a police call box at Front and Market streets in 1959. Authorities urged citizens to utilize the 78 boxes placed throughout the city.
Courtesy Democrat and Chronicle archives

BELOW: Water enthusiasts find the latest facilities to change into swimsuits at Cobbs Hill Park in 1952. During World War II the park had been used as a prisoner-of-war camp. *Courtesy Democrat and Chronicle archives*

LEFT: Construction of the Community War Memorial in June 1954. This aerial photo shows the steel skeleton and the pattern of progress as roofing is put in place. The building was approximately 35 percent completed at this time, with construction moving along just about on schedule. The building was slated for completion by July 1955. Court Street is at left and Broad Street is at right. *Courtesy Local History Division, Central Library of Rochester and Monroe County*

BOTTOM LEFT: Construction of the Community War Memorial on Nov. 30, 1954. *Courtesy Local History Division, Central Library of Rochester and Monroe County*

BELOW: Dedication of the Community War Memorial in September 1954. Mayor Peter Barry is shown speaking on stage.
Courtesy Local History Division, Central Library of Rochester and Monroe County

ABOVE: Bernie Hamilton and Vonnie Hamilton's wedding day at Holy Rosary Church, Feb.7, 1953. *Courtesy M. Yvonne Holman Hamilton*

TOP LEFT: Have you been a good boy? Uh-huh! Christmas in 1952 at E.W. Edwards & Son department store on Main Street. *Courtesy Steve Ford*

TOP RIGHT: Rochester soldiers, from left, Cpls. John Capizzi, Dan Casey and Ed Carroll, hold up their copy of the *Democrat and Chronicle* that they received while serving in Korea in June 1953. The three received their copy of the *Democrat and Chronicle* each day thanks to Casey's uncle, George Monahan. *Courtesy Dan Casey*

ABOVE: James A. Hard before his death at the age of 111 in Rochester. Born in Victor, Hard was one of the last surviving combat veterans of the Civil War, outliving all but one of the 2,675,000 Union soldiers. Hard enlisted in the Union Army four days after the attack on Fort Sumter. As a private in the 32nd New York Infantry, he fought in the Battles of Bull Run, Fredericksburg, Chancellorsville, South Mountain and Antietam. He was the oldest male buried in Mount Hope Cemetery. *Courtesy Democrat and Chronicle archives*

LEFT: In the back yard of their home at 202 Thorncliffe Drive, in west Irondequoit, are Gerard and Roseanne Spindler in 1952. *Courtesy Roseanne Spindler Lawrence*

ABOVE: Josephine "Jo" and Richard "Dick" Power in front of St. Patrick's Church on Sept. 18, 1954.
Courtesy Richard Power

TOP LEFT: Joan Crawford arrives at the Rochester-Monroe County Airport for the Festival of Film Artists for the "George Awards," presented at the George Eastman House on Oct. 26, 1957. *Courtesy Democrat and Chronicle archives*

BOTTOM LEFT: Helen Kenyon Jenkins in her prom dress for graduation night at John Marshall High School, 1956. *Courtesy Dave Howard*

BOTTOM MIDDLE: James J. McManus at his home in Rochester, circa 1950. He died in 1956.
Courtesy Michael McManus

BELOW: Girl Scouts of East Rochester and Webster look for familiar landmarks in an aerial photograph mosaic detailing city streets at the George Eastman House on Jan. 27, 1957. *Courtesy Democrat and Chronicle archives*

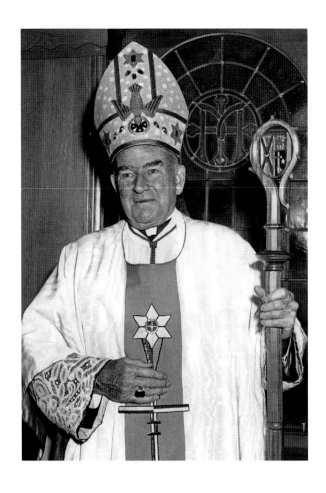

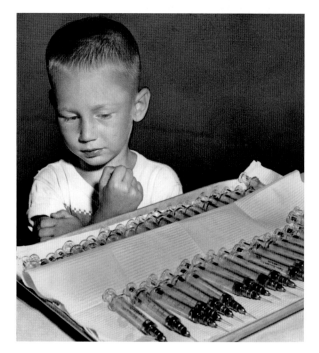

ABOVE: Bishop James E. Kearney on the eve of his 75th birthday, Oct. 27, 1959. *Courtesy Local History Division, Central Library of Rochester and Monroe County*

TOP RIGHT: Mary Ann Burke, 6, kindergarten pupil at School No. 30, takes her Sabin polio vaccine while classmate Deborah Di Angelo, 6, "opens up" too on May 17, 1960. *Courtesy Democrat and Chronicle archives*

RIGHT: Luxury apartments located at 1600 East Ave., circa 1959. *Courtesy Democrat and Chronicle archives*

FAR RIGHT: John Dangler, 4, looks uncertainly at an array of hypodermic needles at the polio clinic at Immaculate Conception School on Aug. 28, 1959. *Courtesy Democrat and Chronicle archives*

ABOVE: This apartment development known as 1000 East Avenue typified changing architectural style on "The Avenue" in December 1961. *Courtesy Democrat and Chronicle archives*

LEFT: Breaking ground for the new Holy Trinity Baptist Church at 397 North St., Aug. 11, 1960. Pictured from left are Rose Beaman, Lansing Cummings, 8, Vice Mayor Joseph Farbo and the Rev. Milton L. Daniels. *Courtesy Democrat and Chronicle archives*

ABOVE: Arthur Farrer stands aboard the fire boat he designed and built in 1960. It was intended to be used on the Irondequoit Bay by the Point Pleasant Fire Department. *Courtesy Democrat and Chronicle archives*

TOP RIGHT: The wrecking begins on the triangle where the Liberty Pole Green would eventually stand. This shot was taken from the top of the Security Trust building on East Avenue and Main Street, Nov. 20, 1964. *Courtesy Democrat and Chronicle archives*

RIGHT: Ironworker Ron Curtiss rides aloft in his bosun's chair. He welds and connects sections making up the steel shaft of the Liberty Pole on Nov. 6, 1965. *Courtesy Democrat and Chronicle archives*

FAR RIGHT: A demonstration on May 7, 1965, at the War Memorial by the Rochester Citizens Against Vietnam group. *Courtesy Democrat and Chronicle archives*

OPPOSITE: Ross Anderson, 63, leads peace marchers, including a number of local residents, toward the city limits along Buffalo Road on June 19, 1963. He had been marching with the demonstration since it had begun in Cleveland, Ohio, in May. *Courtesy Democrat and Chronicle archives*

ABOVE: Buster Keaton, second from left, continues his deadpan comedy routine during the wait for a west-bound plane at the Rochester-Monroe County airport. Others in the group, from left, included cameraman Hal Rosson, Mrs. Keaton, director Marshall Neilan and Brig. Gen. Oscar Solbert (the first director of the George Eastman house), who accompanied his guest stars to the airport, Nov. 21, 1955. Keaton had won a "George Award" at the First Annual George Eastman Festival of FIlm Arts in 1956. *Courtesy Democrat and Chronicle archives*

TOP RIGHT: A view of the city's controversial Liberty Pole Green at Main and North streets. This view is of the frost-bitten fountain. City officials said the icicles formed when the fountain's feed lines froze, Nov. 21, 1966. *Courtesy Democrat and Chronicle archives*

BOTTOM RIGHT: The newly built and completed Liberty Pole Green in the John F. Kennedy Square in downtown Rochester, circa 1966. *Courtesy Democrat and Chronicle archives*

FAR RIGHT: Trenton Jackson, an University of Illinois sprinter, had hopes of adding a gold medal to his trophy case prior to competing in Tokyo Olympics in the fall of 1964. The former Franklin High School star trained at the University of Rochester the previous summer. In 1961, Trenton tied the 100-meter-dash high school world record set by Jesse Owens, with a time of 9.4 seconds. *Courtesy Democrat and Chronicle archives*

BELOW: The Dick Barone Quartet poses at Edgewater Restaurant & Party House on Edgemere Drive off Lake Ontario. From left are Tom DiGrazia, John Tucker, Dick Barone and Tony Coppola. *Courtesy Tony Coppola*

TOP LEFT: Bishop Fulton J. Sheen, celebrates his 50 years as a Roman Catholic priest, Sept. 20, 1969. Sheen, bishop of Rochester from 1966-1969, was a pioneer televangelist, using his television shows Life is Worth Living and The Fulton Sheen Program to spread the Gospel. *Courtesy Democrat and Chronicle archives*

FAR TOP LEFT: John T. Nothnagle, a local Realtor, who introduced his "Gallery of Homes" in 1950. This photo was taken in 1967. *Courtesy Democrat and Chronicle archives*

BOTTOM LEFT: Janet and Karen Peck get a treat from Skippy the ice cream man after dinner on a hot summer day in Greece in 1966.
Courtesy Karen Ogle and Janet Chippero

FAR BOTTOM LEFT: Cousins play while the adults have a chance to catch up. From bottom to top are Karen, Debbie, Janet and Barb Peck in 1966.
Courtesy Karen Ogle and Janet Chippero

OPPOSITE: Radio station WIRQ-FM opened its season on Oct. 5, 1966, and was carrying live broadcasts of all home sporting events. In the mornings the staff used the Irondequoit High School public address system for announcements. The station had a frequency of 90.9 megacycles and a range of 20 miles. Most of the 30 staff members were in radio and workshop courses. Members shown, from left, are program director Paul Fessbender, chief engineer Richard Wetherald, general manager Michael Denesha and newscaster Howard Snow. *Courtesy Democrat and Chronicle archives*

ABOVE: Margaret "Peggy" Morris, Bishop James E. Kearney, and Joe Ryan during a visit to the bishop's residence on East Avenue.
Courtesy Joe Ryan

TOP RIGHT: Sam Lombardo sings with the Edison Tech singers at Bausch & Lomb cafeteria, Jan. 7, 1950.
Courtesy Sam and Josephine Lombardo

BOTTOM RIGHT: Mrs. Amo Kreiger, Honeoye Falls Village Historian, checks up on a flour dresser at the new Mill Restaurant in Honeoye Falls in 1969. Interested in her findings are Ed Trenholm, owner and manager of The Mill and Squire J. Kingston, mayor of Honeoye Falls. The historic mill was among Monroe County's and the nation's most active flour mills, which would be retained as part of The Mill's decor. Tenholm leased The Mill from Honeoye Falls.
Courtesy Democrat and Chronicle archives

FAR RIGHT: Marchers make their way down Court Street near the Community War Memorial after the death of the Rev. Martin Luther King Jr. in April 1968. *Courtesy Democrat and Chronicle archives*

Disasters

Once the seasonal floodwaters of Genesee River were tamed by the Mount Morris Dam in 1949, natural disasters – save for a periodic blizzard or ice storm – were few and far between.

Against the backdrop of three major wars, accidents caused by man or the failure of technology took center stage. Fires, gas explosions and an airliner crash were all disasters that challenged our ability to respond and prompted new preventive and safety measures. Rochesterians showed that most often in the worst of times, the best of human nature comes through as neighbors help each other pick up the pieces and move on.

Although Rochester had the lowest unemployment rate in the state, many black Rochesterians felt disenfranchised with respect to their education and economic opportunities. For three days and two nights in July 1964, thousands of Rochester's African American residents rioted in the streets of the city's low-income neighborhoods. In the stifling summer heat, rioters smashed storefront windows, looted neighborhood merchants and clashed with police, exposing the city's long-simmering racial tensions.

The process of healing began with bringing the black community together and giving its members a voice, as the city struggled to address the root causes of the disaster.

LEFT: A huge column of smoke rises from the Wegmans warehouse blaze as hundreds of curious onlookers crowd around the nearby mounds of earth at the Eastern Expressway and Can of Worms construction site on May 17, 1961. This view is from the railroad side looking southeasterly, with East Avenue at left.
Courtesy Democrat and Chronicle archives

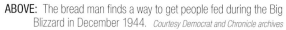

ABOVE: The bread man finds a way to get people fed during the Big Blizzard in December 1944. *Courtesy Democrat and Chronicle archives*

TOP RIGHT: The Four Corners of downtown Rochester as they appeared in December 1944, the day of the Big Blizzard, when transportation and business were halted for 24 hours. *Courtesy Democrat and Chronicle archives*

BOTTOM RIGHT: Motorists struggle to maneuver a car in the snow at the Public Market on March 6, 1947. Henry R. Stevens, market master, said the condition was typical after such a heavy snowfall. *Courtesy Democrat and Chronicle archives*

FAR RIGHT: Firefighters, up to their shins in water, battle a four-alarm blaze on Commercial and Verona streets in 1949. Twenty-one firefighters were injured and two pieces of apparatus were destroyed on June 20, the fire. *Courtesy Democrat and Chronicle archives*

LEFT: Gathering for safety in the Brighton School No. 1 yard are high school and grade school pupils. Clouds of smoke rise in the background caused by a gas explosion that took the lives of three and caused a staggering financial loss in the 12 Corners neighborhoods. The pupils were held until it was certain they would not be exposed to danger going home, Sept. 21, 1951. *Courtesy Democrat and Chronicle archives*

BOTTOM LEFT: Leveled homes on both sides of Antlers Drive are shown in a photo taken from a helicopter that flew over the scene of the Brighton disaster in Sept. of 1951. Antlers Drive was one of the hardest-hit streets. *Courtesy Democrat and Chronicle archives*

BELOW: A funeral procession for Mary Anne and William J. Maas, victims of the Brighton disaster in September 1951, approaches the entrance of Our Lady of Lourdes Church. Schoolmates were the bearers. The sidewalk was lined by officials from the town of Brighton and Rochester Gas and Electric Corp. *Courtesy Democrat and Chronicle archives*

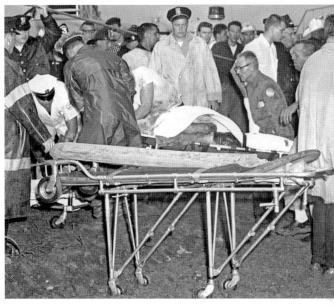

ABOVE: A body of one of the passengers from the Mohawk Airlines Flight 112 plane crash is moved from the scene, July 1963.
Courtesy Democrat and Chronicle archives

TOP LEFT: Aftermath of the Mohawk Airlines Flight 112 plane crash in early July 1963, which killed seven passengers.
Courtesy Democrat and Chronicle archives

BOTTOM LEFT: The man in charge of the crash probe from Mohawk Airlines Flight 112 was William L. Lamb, seen on the right. He confers with a member of his team, Robert H. Mauerman in July 1963.
Courtesy Democrat and Chronicle archives

OPPOSITE LEFT: Onlookers who usually gather to watch construction progress on the War Memorial got something new to look at when flames broke out amid jammed logs in the Genesee River bed below the Broad Street bridge. Firefighter Daniel Jerzak is pictured fighting the blaze as traffic roared by above, Oct. 15, 1953.
Courtesy Local History Division, Central Library of Rochester and Monroe County

OPPOSITE TOP RIGHT: Billows of heavy smoke roll over the North Side area on Aug. 7, 1956, when a fire burns out the warehouse of J. H. Goldberg Furniture Co. at 64-66 Hanover St. The multiple-alarm fire was fueled by tons of mattresses stored in the warehouse.
Courtesy Democrat and Chronicle archives

OPPOSITE MIDDLE RIGHT: An interior shot of Temple Beth El, which was destroyed by fire, Jan. 23, 1960. *Courtesy Local History Division, Central Library of Rochester and Monroe County*

OPPOSITE BOTTOM RIGHT: The last remaining smoke from the fire that all but destroyed the Park Avenue synagogue of Temple Beth El on Meigs Street and Park Avenue on Jan. 23, 1960.
Courtesy Local History Division, Central Library of Rochester and Monroe County

ABOVE: Aftermath of the helicopter crash on Clarissa Street, which occurred on July 26, 1964, during the race riots that shook the city. Three people were killed in the crash, the pilot and two residents of a home on Clarissa. *Courtesy Democrat and Chronicle archives*

LEFT: A view of North Clinton Avenue, looking north, following the race riots in Rochester, July 25, 1964. A confrontation between police and dancers led to looting and rioting that continued through the next night and spread throughout the city's Third and Seventh Wards. The State Police and National Guard were called in to restore order. By the time it ended, four people were dead, 350 were injured, and more than 800, mostly black people, had been arrested. *Courtesy Democrat and Chronicle archives*

TOP RIGHT: Joseph Avenue, in the aftermath of the race riots, July 25, 1964. *Courtesy Democrat and Chronicle archives*

BOTTOM RIGHT: New York State Troopers take a man into custody on July 24 1964. Nearly 1,000 people were arrested and four are killed during three days of race riots in two Rochester neighborhoods, 1964. *Courtesy Democrat and Chronicle archives.*

BELOW: It was both hot and muggy during the tense weekend in July 1964, which forced kids to sleep on mattresses on the floor. The rioting and frequent gunshots also made it very dangerous to open windows, adding to the difficult conditions. *Courtesy Democrat and Chronicle archives*

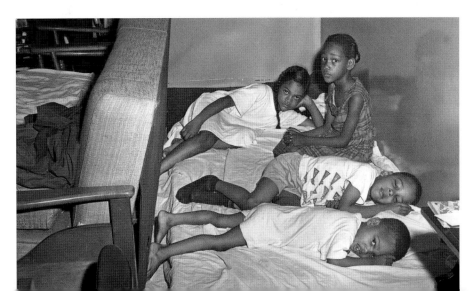

ABOVE: Volunteer fire chiefs, in white coats, confer in front of the rubble of a supermarket and lodge building in Hilton, 1965. *Courtesy Democrat and Chronicle archives*

TOP: Dispatchers at the Rochester Police Bureau handle emergency calls during the blackout on Nov. 9, 1965, caused by an electrical power failure. *Courtesy Democrat and Chronicle archives*

RIGHT: Passengers arriving at the Monroe County Airport walk in the light provided by trucks in the background during the blackout on Nov. 9, 1965, caused by an electrical power failure. *Courtesy Democrat and Chronicle archives*

FAR RIGHT: An aerial view shows firemen battling the multimillion-dollar blaze, that raged out of control for six hours on March 21, 1965, in Hilton's business area. *Courtesy Democrat and Chronicle archives*

Recreation & Celebration

The main source of recreation in the 1940s was the movies. The Office of War proclaimed the industry as "an essential industry for morale and propaganda." Rochester, of course, had a role to play. Kodak's motion picture film set the standard for the industry.

Rochester became the envy of many midsized cities as it grew and supported numerous world-class cultural institutions. These included the Rochester Philharmonic Orchestra, the George Eastman House, the Memorial Art Gallery, the Strong Museum, the Rochester Museum & Science Center and the Strasenburgh Planetarium.

As the 1940s gave way to the 1950s, Rochesterians found themselves with more leisure time, greater prosperity and more mobility with their new automobiles. Beaches, parks and festivals became a staple of weekend recreation. On almost any summer weekend, one needn't travel far to find a parade, a ball game or a chance to play.

In 1888, nurserymen George Ellwanger and Patrick Barry endowed the Flower City with 20 acres of gentle hills known as Highland Park. While noted as one of the nation's first municipal arboretums, it gained fame as the site of Rochester's most enduring rite of spring. The Lilac Festival is the oldest festival of its kind in North America, a celebration of floral splendor that draws visitors from around the globe.

LEFT: Winners of the "George" award at the George Eastman Theater, from left, front to back are Peverell Marley, Harold Lloyd, George Folsey, Gloria Swanson, Lillian Gish, Janey Gaynor, Mary Pickford, Josef von Sternberg, Arthur Edeson, Richard Barthelmess, James Wong Howe, Ramon Novarro, William Daniels, Lee Garmes, Frank Borzage, Charles Rosher and Maurice Chevalier, 1957.
Courtesy Democrat and Chronicle archives

ABOVE: Clifford "Skip" Goodrich, first on the left, a prominent golfer in the area, wins the championship at the Brook-Lea Open, August 1940. *Courtesy Dennis Patton*

BELOW: Reed family sleigh ride in the 1940s. *Courtesy James J. Reed*

ABOVE: Sam Lombardo sits on horseback on Zimmer Street, 1940.
Courtesy Sam and Josephine Lombardo

TOP LEFT: Ernest "Bob" Hart and Helen Hart Bischoping, on horseback, out on the Hart Farm at 4201 Buffalo Road, November 1942. *Courtesy Helen Bischoping & Noreen Crouse*

TOP RIGHT: James Hackett and sister Nancy at their grandmother's house at 145 Masseth St. in 1944. *Courtesy Nancy E. Hackett Steger*

OPPOSITE: Dennis Stewart Patton, on left, and his sister Christine E. Patton, sit along the shoreline off Lake Ontario in Hamlin during the summer of 1938. This picture was taken in front of the summer cottage of their maternal grandparents, Walter and Rose Goodrich. *Courtesy Dennis Patton*

ABOVE: The wedding day of Bill and Rita Almy, couple on the right, with best man Mike Sheer and maid of honor Marion Lyons, 1944. *Courtesy Ken and Mary Feicht*

BELOW: World War II veterans participate in their first Memorial Day parade, May 31, 1945. *Courtesy Local History Division, Central Library of Rochester and Monroe County*

ABOVE: There wasn't a back yard big enough to accommodate everybody, so residents from Sixth Street used the pavement for a community dinner celebrating the Japanese surrender on Aug. 14, 1945. *Courtesy Democrat and Chronicle archives*

BELOW: It was before dawn and a time when Rochester is normally asleep, but this crowd didn't care how much noise it made. Neither did anyone else. The news overjoyed everyone on Aug. 14, 1945; Japan had surrendered. *Courtesy Democrat and Chronicle archives*

ABOVE: For eight hours beginning with the normally quiet time of 3 a.m., Rochester's downtown streets resounded with whooping and cheering when news of Japan's surrender was announced on Aug. 14, 1945. *Courtesy Local History Division, Central Library of Rochester and Monroe County*

LEFT: A group gathers in the streets following V-J Day, Aug. 14, 1945, to express their gratitude for the news of the end of the bloodiest conflict of World War II. Many took time to pause amid the rain in victory celebration and to unite in giving thanks to God for the end of the war. *Courtesy Local History Division, Central Library of Rochester and Monroe County*

BELOW: Diane Selg reads the headlines about the war's end in 1945. *Courtesy Diane Drysdale*

ABOVE: A 50th anniversary party for Wiley and Jessie Almy on East Avenue in Brighton, 1946. *Courtesy Ken and Mary Feicht*

TOP RIGHT: Rochester's National Basketball League, The Royals, entry heads for Seton Hall College, New Jersey, to open practice for the coming season. From left are George Glamack, Arnie Johnson, manager Less Harrison, Jack Harrison, Al Cervi, and Jim Quinlan, October 14, 1946. *Courtesy Local History Division, Central Library of Rochester and Monroe County*

BOTTOM RIGHT: C.K. Flint, general manager of Kodak Park Athletic Association International Softball League, in the back of the car on his way to throw out the first ball of the opening season. The game was at Kodak Park on Lake Avenue in 1947. *Courtesy Bill Tribelhorn*

OPPOSITE: Members of Forman-Kramb Post, American Legion, keeping perfect step, march past the Times-Union Building. They formed a colorful part of the Memorial Day Parade on May 31, 1946. *Courtesy Local History Division, Central Library of Rochester and Monroe County*

BELOW: Women who served in World War II make their first appearance in numbers since V-J Day during Rochester's Memorial Day parade in 1946. *Courtesy Local History Division, Central Library of Rochester and Monroe County*

ABOVE: The Tops team of the Kodak Park Athletic Association, K. P. A. A., youth softball program, John Marshall High School, 1947. The 11-year-old boys are from the 10th and 23rd wards and won the pony league. *Courtesy Reyton Wojnowski*

TOP LEFT: The Rochester Royals' leading cripples, Arnie Johnson, right, and Fuzzy Levane, center, are shown with Bob Davies, who points to Fuzzy's broken nose and Arnie's foot, which is also broken, Feb. 23, 1947. *Courtesy Local History Division, Central Library of Rochester and Monroe County*

BOTTOM LEFT: Among the hundreds who partook of the Rochester Gas and Electric Corp.'s birthday cake on October 30, 1948, was Mayor Samuel B. Dicker, who is shown here getting his cake from Robert E. Ginna, left, vice president of the company, and Councilman Norman Kreckman, president of the Electrical Association of Rochester. The city officials presided at the cake-cutting to celebrate the corporation's centennial. The cake contained 15, 618 raisins and was the subject of a guessing contest won by Mrs. Harold Wiley of Avon, who guessed 15, 621 raisins. She won a radio.
Courtesy Democrat and Chronicle archives

OPPOSITE: Winner in the invitational tournament in September 1947, Eleanor Cole, right, former city champ, who defeated Pam Estes, Syracuse city champ. *Courtesy Local History Division, Central Library of Rochester and Monroe County*

ABOVE: Members of the Barbed Wire Club re-create the historic flag raising at Iwo Jima on board a float in the Rochester Memorial Day parade in 1949. *Courtesy Local History Division, Central Library of Rochester and Monroe County*

TOP RIGHT: When television came to Rochester in June 1949, Donald Poole, one of the corps of TV cameramen, was at his post in the balcony of the Chamber of Commerce, recording events at the speakers' table during the ceremony. *Courtesy Democrat and Chronicle archives*

BOTTOM RIGHT: The first airplane to participate in a Rochester parade was this one, entered by the Air Force Post, American Legion in 1949. *Courtesy Local History Division, Central Library of Rochester and Monroe County*

OPPOSITE: The first television program to originate in Rochester was staged on April 27, 1949, at Hotel Sheraton, directed by WHTM. One of the 11 acts in the variety show is shown. Program director John Crosby crouches, at right, while Charles Snyder operates the camera. The program was enacted on the roof of the hotel and telecast to the audience in the ballroom 10 floors down. The event was sponsored by Bickford Bros. Inc., distributors in Western New York for RCA Victor. The program did not go on the air for general reception. Television officially came to Rochester at 1 p.m. on June 11, 1949, when the city's first television station, WHAM-TV, began broadcasting during a ceremony at the Chamber of Commerce banquet hall. *Courtesy Democrat and Chronicle archives*

142

ABOVE: Members of Cub Scout pack 81 on stage at the Kodak Park Elementary School, present their skit for fellow scouts at a Christmas party, December 1949. Dennis A. Patton, in the straw hat, leads his fellow Cubs in a rendition of "Old MacDonald had a Farm." Others are unidentified. *Courtesy Dennis Patton*

BELOW: Arlene Giebel LaBounty, takes her sons Val and his new baby brother, Scott, on a sleigh ride through Arlene's parent's backyard at 415 Lake Ave., Rochester. The picture was taken during the winter of 1951-1952. *Courtesy Renee LaBounty Ange*

ABOVE: Mrs. George Trainor of Oak Hill received the WRDGA championship trophy on July 29, 1951, from Otto Shutts, president of Oak Hill, after winning her eighth WRDGA crown. It was her fifth straight triumph in the tournament. She defeated Mrs. Morton Baum of Irondequoit. *Courtesy Local History Division, Central Library of Rochester and Monroe County*

LEFT: Thelma Drury and her clarinet are ready to march in the Memorial Day Parade in 1951. *Courtesy Thelma Peck*

OPPOSITE: Kodak Park Athletic Association softball team, The Wolverines, 1951. The Wolverines were Colonial League Champions in 1951. *Courtesy Dave Howard*

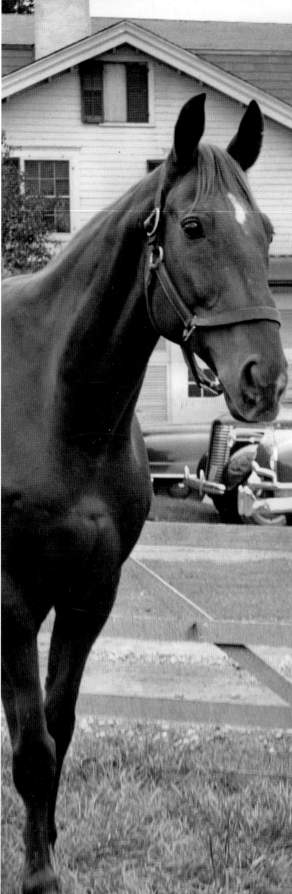

ABOVE: Eight of the city's 10 ice skating rinks were opened officially on Jan. 7, 1953, and it didn't take youngsters long to hear the good news and flock to the rinks. This group is at Cobbs Hill Park.
Courtesy Democrat and Chronicle archives

RIGHT: The busiest season in the 75-year history of the Genesee Valley Hunt would culminate in just a few weeks when the annual Hunt Ball at Big Tree Inn in Geneseo, Livingston County, would bring together Hunt members and their guests for the festive evening diamond jubilee celebration on Oct. 27, 1951. Two final events were scheduled to bring sleek hunters and expert riders to the rolling countryside of Livingston County. Gathering at the Homestead to talk over details for these three Hunt events are William P. Wadsworth, master of the Hunt, left; Hubert W. Chanler, Mrs. Chanler, Mrs. Thomas C. T. Buckley and Mr. Buckley. The Homestead was a manor house on the estate of the late Maj. Austin W. Wadsworth, who introduced the ancient sport in the Genesee Valley, and the home of his son, William.
Courtesy Democrat and Chronicle archives

ABOVE: Donald Brodie shows off his catch from an ice fishing outing at Buttonwood Creek, February 1953. *Courtesy Carol DeBellis*

RIGHT: Ladies Bowling Banquet at Sheehans in the spring of 1953. From left are June Utter; unidentified; Mary Power; Mary Sheehan, sponsor; Josephine Power; Geraldine Utter; and unidentified.
Courtesy Sharon DiFelice

ABOVE: Sharon DiFelice and Peggy Hamm, sisters, with Santa in Sibley's Toyland, December 1954. *Courtesy Sharon DiFelice*

TOP LEFT: It had been a long time since most of Rochester had seen a horse-drawn ice cream wagon. But to youngsters in the North Street and Clifford Avenue area, Carmen Sorce and his horse and wagon were a familiar sight in the summer in 1954. The kids called Sorce "The Lemonade Man." Sorce sold frozen lemonade in cones. He is shown serving Yvonne Hopp as Rosario Furia waits his turn. Sorce had plans to retire from the business at the close of the summer that year. *Courtesy Democrat and Chronicle archives*

BOTTOM LEFT: Gov. Thomas E. Dewey cuts the ribbon at the Thruway stretch opening ceremony at Le Roy on Aug. 26, 1954. From left are John E. Johnston of Le Roy, state assemblyman; R. Burdell Bixby, Dewey's secretary and secretary-treasurer of the State Thruway Authority; Oswald D. Heck, speaker of the Assembly; Mrs. Dewey; Walter Mahoney of Buffalo, acting lieutenant governor; ribbon cutter Dewey; Bertam D. Tallamy, authority chairman; and Mrs. Tallamy. *Courtesy Democrat and Chronicle archives*

OPPOSITE: With the oompah of bands (in this case Slager Post Band), the baseball season was launched in the chilly atmosphere on April 24, 1952, with a parade, luncheon and, of course, a ball game. The Red Wings won. *Courtesy Local History Division, Central Library of Rochester and Monroe County*

ABOVE: High school members of the East High Buddies pose for a shot at "Chuck" Higbies Sporting Goods and Sportswear Center in Rochester, 1955. *Courtesy Carmen Santora*

TOP RIGHT: Five-year-old Billy Pagano watches a Naval Reserve group pass during a parade in June 1954 to mark the arrival of Gov. Thomas E. Dewey's Thruway cavalcade in Rochester. *Courtesy Local History Division, Central Library of Rochester and Monroe County*

BELOW: The KPAA Rangers baseball team of 1955. *Courtesy Local History Division, Central Library of Rochester and Monroe County*

BELOW: One of the sleekest cars at the Watkins Glen Grand Prix in 1955 was this rare Lotus Mark IX, an aluminum car owned by Len Bastrup of Wilton, Conn. *Courtesy Local History Division, Central Library of Rochester and Monroe County*

TOP LEFT: Shifty Gears, center, official of the Champion Major Softball League, discusses ground rules with Mike Farrell, left, manager of Kodak Park, and Herb Jenning, Hotel DeMay manager, before the opening league game on May 13, 1957, at Kodak Park. Kodak Park took a 5-1 victory. *Courtesy Local History Division, Central Library of Rochester and Monroe County*

BOTTOM LEFT: Frank P. Geraci, Jr., stands in front of a Buick Special wearing a Red Wings uniform and holding a bat in his hand, in Rochester, in 1955. He later became a Monroe County Court judge. *Courtesy Frank P. Geraci, Jr.*

BELOW: Locust Hill Country Club, a few days prior to being dedicated in July 1957. Children and adults didn't wait until the dedication to enjoy the benefits of the new steel pool, the first of its type in the Rochester area. At left is the shower house, with the snack bar inside, and sun deck on top. *Courtesy Local History Division, Central Library of Rochester and Monroe County*

ABOVE: Cynthia and Neil Howk are dressed for fun and snow during the midwinter school break in February 1958. They are in front of their family home off North Winton Road. *Courtesy Cynthia Howk*

OPPOSITE: Carey Brown, left, Gordon Howe and Mayor Peter Barry turn earth for the groundbreaking of the Civic Center in January 1958. *Courtesy Democrat and Chronicle archives*

BELOW: Three members of the Rochester Colonels pro basketball club talk over plans for the season at a luncheon, Sept. 22, 1958, at the Powers Hotel. From left, Arnie Risen, former Royal; Charlie Hoxie and Bo Erias. *Courtesy Local History Division, Central Library of Rochester and Monroe County*

ABOVE: Spectators jam Childrens' Pavilion in Highland Park as Lilac Time opens on May 19, 1960. *Courtesy Democrat and Chronicle archives*

BELOW: Wedding of Helen Jean Hart to Jerome Anthony Bischoping at the St. Pius X Church, Jan. 3, 1959. *Courtesy Helen Bischoping & Noreen Crouse*

MASSAWEPIE
SCOUT 1962 CAMPS
TROOP 242

ABOVE: Itching Palm, Cross Country and Orient Drift, from left, streak across the finish line in the third race as the Finger Lakes track opens in 1962.
Courtesy Democrat and Chronicle archives

LEFT: Boy Scout Troop 242 at Camp Massawepie in St. Lawrence County, in 1962. *Courtesy Bill Tribelhorn*

BELOW: Shortly after its opening in December 1962, the new skating rink in East Rochester's Edmund Lyon Park became a popular place for young and old alike. In the summer months it became a spray pool or roller skating rink. *Courtesy Democrat and Chronicle archives*

ABOVE: The showing of Walt Disney's *Old Yeller* at the RKO Palace in 1963. *Courtesy Democrat and Chronicle archives*

TOP RIGHT: Crowds flock to the Riviera Theater to see the highly popular, *My Fair Lady,* in 1964. *Courtesy Democrat and Chronicle archives*

BOTTOM RIGHT: Enjoying their tricycles on Bryan Street are Sheila Gartland, John Papano, Maria Papano and Patty Gartland, 1963. *Courtesy Edward Gartland*

BELOW: A crowd of 14,215 attends the Wings opening game on April 22, 1961. *Courtesy Democrat and Chronicle archives*

ABOVE: Red Wings general manager George Sisler Jr., left, and board Chairman Morrie Silver discuss the team's issues at the Powers conference in 1965. *Courtesy Local History Division, Central Library of Rochester and Monroe County*

TOP LEFT: Rochester Red Wings baseball team, 1964. *Courtesy Local History Division, Central Library of Rochester and Monroe County*

BOTTOM LEFT: The American Bowling Congress champions of 1963. The only one identified is Clifford Goodrich, second from the right. *Courtesy Dennis Patton*

ABOVE: State conservative party chairman, Kieran O'Doherty and Monroe County conservative party chairman, Raymond Lee Snider are interviewed by *Democrat and Chronicle* reporter following the party meeting on July 11, 1962. Snider later served as Republican conservative party candidate for county legislator. *Courtesy Raymond Lee Sider*

TOP RIGHT: Mayor Frank Lamb tests out a new swing set on the Syracuse Street playground, on May 11, 1969. Behind him is the Playmobile, Rochester's first mobile recreation vehicle, was created in 1966 to bring recreation to areas of the inner city. Sponsored by the Rochester Jaycees, it featured puppet shows, music, crafts, volleyball basketball and a variety of other activities. *Courtesy Democrat and Chronicle archives*

BELOW: The Hilton Central Band strikes up a tune in prelude to the dedication of the Hilton Post Office on June 24, 1968. *Courtesy Democrat and Chronicle archives*

ABOVE: Sacred Heart Cathedral Women's Bowling League in 1967. Shown here, from left, are Delores, Joyce Lesczinski, Grace and Sophia. *Courtesy Joyce Lesczinski*

RIGHT: The community gathers for a Rochester Philharmonic Orchestra concert at the Highland Park Bowl in 1968. *Courtesy Democrat and Chronicle archives*

Index